IN SEARCH OF

CIVILIZATIONS

IN SEARCH OF
THE FIRST CIVILIZATIONS

MICHAEL WOOD

BBC
BOOKS

First published in hardback 1992
This paperback edition first published 2005

Published by BBC Books, BBC Worldwide Ltd,
Woodlands, 80 Wood Lane, London W12 0TT

ISBN 0 563 52266 6

Commissioning editors: Sheila Ableman and Sally Potter
Project editors: Katy Lord and Martin Redfern
Designer: Linda Blakemore
Cartographer: Eugene Fleury

Printed and bound in Great Britain by Mackays of Chatham
Colour separations by Butler & Tanner, Frome

CONTENTS

For Rebecca

PREFACE

IN THE YEAR 1000, if you were a traveller or trader with the contacts and the curiosity, you could have seen all the ancient civilizations of the Old World at the very height of their traditional culture. If you were a Western European you would have needed the Arabic language too, for this was the lingua franca of sailors between the Mediterranean and the Indian Ocean. But with spoken Arabic (and a lot of luck to avoid pirates, shipwreck and disease) you could have hitched a series of passages from Anglo-Saxon England to the Yellow Sea, bartering your way along well-trodden trade routes: with Arabs in the Arabian Sea, Tamils across the Indian Ocean to Indonesia, and then Chinese captains who traded the whole vast area between Mombasa and Japan. And what a wonderful journey! You could have visited Byzantium, Cairo, Abbasid Baghdad, Cholan South India, Cambodia and Sung dynasty China. These civilizations had arisen in the Bronze Age. The oldest had developed their religion and philosophy, science and technology over four millennia, and all were now at the peak of their achievement in arts, science and humanistic culture. You could have visited glittering courts, magnificent churches, mosques and temples, and seen wonderful treasures of art and architecture. If there is one moment in time to which one might wish to travel, it would surely be this.

Move on five hundred years, and the picture changes. The descendants of the ancient civilizations are still there in Persia, Ming China, and Moghul India. But by 1500 AD, the axis of history is shifting, its centre of gravity no longer in its Asiatic heartland. As we see it now, the opening up of the sea route to India and the discovery of the New World were indeed, as Adam Smith said, 'the greatest events in the history of the world.' At the time the idea would have been laughed at by Chinese mandarins at court in Peking. Their ships had, after all, already explored the African coast, rounded the Cape of Good Hope and landed in Australia. Huge fleets with giant ships, dwarfing the boats of

Columbus, Magellan and Vasco de Gama; vessels equipped with stern rudders, the compass and gunpowder, with shipboard kitchen gardens growing fresh vegetables. But history was in fact against them. In the 1520s and 30s the empires of the Aztecs and the Incas in Mexico and Peru were overthrown by European adventurers armed with new technology. The European appropriation of the American continent and its natural resources rapidly followed, with the virtual extermination of the native population. This set the stage for the era of European world domination, at the end of which we still live. The colonial epoch has seen the demolition of most of the traditional civilizations and societies, ending in the twentieth century with the disintegration of imperial China and the undermining of the last traditional Muslim civilization in Persia. Of all the classical cultures, perhaps only the Tamil survived in anything like a recognizable form at the end of the twentieth century. Now, I suspect we have reached the point of no return in the advance of globalization and modernism. The battles against modernity fought in the nineteenth and twentieth centuries – the Mayan Revolt, the Iranian Revolution, the Hindu revival are only three of the most typical – now look like a rearguard action as the global hegemony of the free market and TV culture scrubs away encoded identities built up over several millennia.

This trajectory is the background to this book, and has become all the more clear in the years since it was first written. Expanded from the scripts of a series of film essays, it attempts a sketch of how we got here: the first 5000 years of civilization. It is a portrait of the first civilizations and their continuing legacy, beginning with the revolution which took place in the Fertile Crescent five thousand years ago when human beings first began to live in cities. It focuses on the city civilizations which developed independently in Iraq, Egypt, India, China and Central America: the ancient civilizations which made us what we are – in our modes of thinking, in our religious beliefs, in our ways of organizing human society – and which still affect the lives of everyone on earth today.

The films involved long journeys inside these cultures. We stayed in mudbrick villages in the wheatfields of northern China and in tents among millions of pilgrims at India's Kumbh Mela; we slept in the reed huts of the Marsh Arabs in South Iraq. These were the kind of journeys and experiences which opened new vistas on the relative importance of one's own culture and history. To find oneself, for example, in the old Jewish quarter in Kaifeng in China in the place which led the world in industry, science and printing in the tenth century; to listen to Tamil oduvars singing sixth-century hymns to a huge and appreciative festival audience in the enormous temple at Chidambaram in South India; to be present at Momostenago in Highland Guatemala on the festival of 'Eight Monkey' when new Mayan shamans are initiated who will keep their pre-Christian calendar: such experiences make history come alive in a way which no book can. And of course they also offer an entirely different perspective on the world. China's history, to use an example almost too obvious to need stating, is as rich and diverse as that of the West.

Visits to Baghdad on the eve of the Gulf War were equally illuminating and exciting. There are very few surviving physical remains of that most astonishing epoch of pluralist culture which flourished in Baghdad also in that same tenth century. But in conversation with Iraqi scholars and friends both there and in exile, I was constantly reminded that the brilliant literature and philosophy of that time is still common currency in educated Arabic culture in a way that comparable material in the West simply is not. We all have much to learn about, and from, each other's civilizations.

The word 'civilization' is used throughout this book. It is a problematic term these days with its connotations of racial and cultural superiority, as when Western politicians speak of the 'civilized world', when they mean their own liberal democratic culture. The definition of civilization commonly used by anthropologists and archaeologists is a material one. For them civilization means, literally, 'life in cities'. We speak of the 'rise of civilization' or the 'first civilizations' on this basis. As we shall see, the moral and spiritual character of the world's early civilizations was very diverse. But their common markers in material terms are virtually universal: cities, bronze technology, writing, great ceremonial buildings, temples, monumental art, hierarchies and class division, all sanctioned by some form of law, and held together by organized military force. Of the six primary civilizations, Iraq, Egypt, India, China, Central America and Peru, only the last, which is not treated in this book, did not develop all these features (most notably, the early Peruvians did not have writing). Nevertheless, these common material factors hide very different conceptions of what civilization actually is, that is, the ultimate goals of organized human life on earth, moral, intellectual, political and spiritual, and therein lies the fascination of this kind of comparative history.

The choice of the civilizations in this book, it should be stressed, depends on the independent rise of large-scale urban life. Hence the exclusion of other no less fascinating cultures, in Japan for example, Cambodia, Crete or West Africa, which are not generally regarded as primary. This point about the independent origins of civilization has particular significance for us now, for only when we look at the beginnings and the long and continuing influence of the first civilizations can we hope to understand what is universally relevant in our own history and what is merely Western idiosyncrasy. Now at the beginning of a new millennium, it is a good time to reflect on the great historical questions raised by the pace of change in our own time. The histories and identities of the civilizations and peoples in this book are in the process of being erased as surely as the rainforests are being felled. One of the great battles of the twenty-first century will be whether these traditional worlds will survive at all in the face of modernism's massive and deliberate assault on the givenness of what has come down to us from the past. If not, we may be the last generation to see much of what is described in this book.

ONE

IRAQ
THE CRADLE OF
CIVILIZATION

IN THE WINTER OF 1849, a young Englishman, William Loftus, led
a small party on horseback south from Baghdad into the plains of
southern Iraq. Once famous as ancient Chaldaea or Babylonia,
the country was now a wasteland of desert and swamps inhabited
by Bedouin or semi-nomadic tribes, who had proved virtually
ungovernable under the long period of Turkish rule in Iraq. The
first part of Loftus' journey led down the palm-fringed banks of
the river Euphrates. There in the decaying mudbrick towns old
communities of Jews and Mandaean baptists lived alongside their
Muslim brethren, still preserving some of the ancient folk
customs of Babylonia. With some trepidation, Loftus entered the
sacred cities of the Shia Muslims, and was deeply impressed by
their strange and forbidding rituals. The sombre and glittering
magnificence of their shrines and their archaic burial rites seemed
to him to hark back to a past older still than Islam. He saw too
communities of Nestorian Christians who traced their presence
in Iraq back to the earliest days of Christianity and whose beliefs
and forms of worship were a far cry from the Roman and
Orthodox churches of the Mediterranean world. Everywhere
were signs of deep continuities. Indeed, all three monotheistic
religions – Judaism, Christianity, and Islam – claimed a point of
origin here in the land of Abraham. For educated Christian
Europeans in the nineteenth century, fascinated by the origins of
their own culture which was now dominant across the world, it
seemed that their roots must lie here, even before the classical

11

legacy of Greece. As Loftus wrote, 'Here from our childhood we have been led to regard as the cradle of the human race.' Here had been the garden of Eden, the tower of Babel, Noah's ark and the great Flood. And here, according to the Book of Genesis, the first cities had been built out of mudbrick, 'in the Land of Shinar,' apparently a garbled recollection of southern Iraq's ancient name, S(h)umer. The author of Genesis even named some of those cities: Babylon, Akkad and Erech.

Much of the deep south of the plain was now covered by swamps, and except in the dry season the heartland of the ancient civilization was only reachable by boat. Its inhabitants were the mysterious Madan, the Marsh Arabs, who lived a semi-aquatic existence on artificial islands, fishing and cultivating the reed beds in their bitumen-covered boats. Guided by them, Loftus crossed 'a dead sea with salt-encrusted shores.' Everywhere he saw the mounds of ancient settlements. He was not the first European to come this way: in the 1750s the German, Karsten Niebuhr, had stayed among the Marsh Arabs, and J. Baillie Fraser in the 1820s had seen some of the sites in the southern plain. But now Loftus was to test the ancient stories by excavation. His goal was 'the most extraordinary and important of all the mounds of Chaldaea,' a place known to the local Arabs as Warka.

'I know of nothing more exciting or impressive,' he wrote later, 'than the first sight of one of these great Chaldaean piles, looming in solitary grandeur from the surrounding plains and marshes; especially in the hazy atmosphere of early morning when its faery-like effect is heightened by mirages, its forms strangely and fantastically magnified, elevating it from the ground and causing it to dance and quiver in the rarefied air.'

Under a scorching sun, and whipped by 'tornadoes of sand', Loftus finally reached the mound of Warka. He was astonished to find a six-mile circuit of walls silted with great dunes of wind-blown sand, but still standing, 50 feet high in places: in the centre huge eroded pyramids of mudbrick had been platforms for the temples of the city gods. 'Of all the desolate sights I ever beheld,' he said later, 'that of Warka incomparably surpasses all.'

Loftus had found the ancient city of Uruk, the Biblical Erech of the Book of Genesis. In the Arabic 'Warka', the local tribes-people had preserved the memory of its ancient name even though the city had been abandoned for over a thousand years. In places the site was over 100 feet deep in debris, the accumulated layers of human habitation. Loftus was able to see that it had been lived in for thousands of years, till well into the first millennium AD when Greeks, Parthians and Sassanian Persians had made their homes there, leaving tell-tale traces in their pottery, coins, burial offerings, and also in their writing. For although Loftus could not have known it, the first proper writing on earth comes from southern Iraq. Indeed it is just conceivable that it was first invented in Uruk itself!

'A thousand thoughts and surmises present themselves to the mind,' wrote Loftus as he surveyed the ruins, 'concerning its past history and origin – its gradual rise and its rapid fall.' Over 150 years on, those questions are still being asked, and with increasing urgency, as we modern people try to understand the causes of the beginning of urban life on earth. For Loftus had found the first true city in the world, a vast and complex living organism which had lasted for millennia before it died. And many of the key questions are still unanswered surrounding that revolutionary period in history which changed the whole history of the planet, for good and ill.

THE BEGINNINGS OF CIVILIZATION

'The land,' as the Sumerians called it, is a flat alluvial plain 300 miles long and never more than 150 miles wide. It was created by the silt of the two rivers, Tigris and Euphrates, which flow down the plain, hence its Greek name Mesopotamia, 'the land between the rivers.' Rising in the hills of Armenia, the Tigris is the bigger, faster and more unpredictable of the two, more dangerous in flood: even in the last hundred years it has devastated Baghdad on several occasions after bursting its banks. The Euphrates is smaller and less violent, and most of the early cities were clustered along its lower course. The two rivers were the foundation of the achievement built up in the south over 150 generations: great brown arteries carrying life-giving silt in their waters, flowing through what in the summer is a burning dun-coloured flat land. Without irrigation, any farming is impossible in such a landscape, and the irrigation necessary to sustain big populations in cities was impossible without large-scale co-operative enterprise. Nor was the plain endowed with any other natural resources: there was little stone, no wood or precious metals. Apart from reeds and palm trees, the only building material was mudbrick, with which the people became brilliantly adept, inventing the dome and the arch and constructing some of the largest and most impressive brick structures in the world.

The creation of an artificial landscape in the southern plain, with the elaborate irrigation systems needed to sustain city civilization, made the Sumerians peculiarly vulnerable to outside attack. This has been one of the key factors in their history. With no natural frontiers, Mesopotamia was always at risk from its neighbours, especially to the east, from the Elamites and, later, the Persians, the ancient enemies from beyond the Zagros mountains which crowd Iraq's eastern flank, forming a harsh rugged plateau, austere and arid, extending as far as Afghanistan and the Indus. Hill peoples against peoples of the plain; nomads against sedentary farmers: these are two of the most ancient confrontations in human history.

To the west and south were the desert peoples, 'people who have never known a city,' as the Sumerians liked to call them, who also mounted periodic raids to plunder the stored wealth of the cities. Such were the perennial equations of Iraqi history. And this age-old drama is still being played out on our TV screens today. The nomads of the desert may no longer be a force to reckon with, but even in the 1980s the population of Mesopotamia fought its wars with its traditional enemies in Persia, and the hill peoples to the north, the Kurds, retreated to their mountains after battles with the despot in Baghdad.

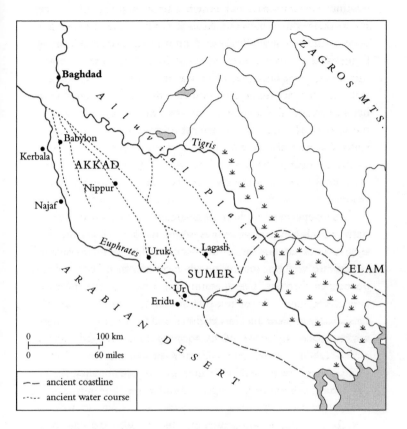

Southern Iraq, showing the old courses of the Tigris and Euphrates. Sumer
extended from Nippur to the sea, then at Ur and Eridu; some of the ancient
cities continued into the Middle Ages, but none is now inhabited.

In landscape and climate, then, we can see the long-term patterns which have shaped the region's history. Against such deep continuities its peoples have lived their lives and created their civilizations which in their turn have risen and fallen. And there is no question that landscape and climate were key determining factors in the rise of civilization. All four great civilizations of the Old World arose on rivers, all of them in a narrow band around 30 degrees latitude in the temperate zone of the northern hemisphere: on the Euphrates and Tigris, the Nile, the Indus, and the Yellow River. In their character they may have differed widely. But in the material basis of their development, they shared very similar conditions and similar concerns.

The first condition of civilization of course is food. Then, as now, cities and large populations cannot exist without the ability to feed people. So the domestication and cultivation of certain staple cereals and grains (such as wheat and barley) was the first step towards large-scale settled societies. The development of agriculture, which made this possible for the first time in human history, seems to have begun around ten to twelve thousand years ago in the wide belt of foothills stretching round the Fertile Crescent, from Palestine, Jordan, Israel and Syria, through south-eastern Turkey, across northern Iraq, and into western Iran. In the eighth millennium BC these Neolithic agricultural communities created small towns such as Jericho in the Jordan valley, which had stone defences enclosing about 11 acres. The remarkable (and still only partially excavated) site at Çatal Hüyük in Anatolia covered 32 acres in the sixth millennium BC, a sizeable place with as many as a thousand houses and five thousand people, looking very much like the little flat-roofed towns to be seen today in the Kurdish uplands.

Nothing is known of the social or political organization of such settlements, but religion may already have been an important element in their rise. At Çatal Hüyük a shrine was identified by the excavator, with evidence of a bull cult and signs of worship of the prehistoric mother goddess who is found throughout ancient Anatolia and the Near East. A recent, spectacular find in the Upper Euphrates valley near Urfa in Turkey may well be the earliest temple yet known. This building, from the eighth millennium BC, was 35 feet square with pillars and a polished gravel and chalk floor. Its kitchen, stores and workshop were reminiscent of later Near Eastern temples and mosques, and winged half-human figures found in the main room strikingly recall the angels and genies of later Near Eastern religious imagery. Another new discovery, at Ain Ghazal in Jordan, also reminds us of the deep continuities in the patterns of ritual and worship in the region. Here near life-sized human images have been uncovered dating from 7000 BC – the oldest statues in the world. Coated with white gypsum plaster, they have the same socketed and black-ringed eyes which were to be characteristic of Mesopotamian cult right down to the Graeco-Roman age and even into the early Christian era.

In Iraq itself agricultural communities were established in the northern hills by the seventh millennium BC; by the sixth millennium they built villages defended with walls of sun-dried bricks. Some of these ancient sites have remained inhabited till today. At Tel Afar, a Turkoman town on the old caravan road from Mosul into Syria, pottery from the fifth millennium BC has been found inside the citadel, and Irbil on its mound near the Great Zab river may be as early. Both are among the longest continuously occupied places on earth. Already, no doubt, as populations slowly expanded, mankind had begun to make its mark on the environment: slashing, burning, cutting down forests, clearing brushwood, leaving that distinctive, bare-ribbed hilly landscape of Eastern Anatolia and Kurdistan we see today. The soil thus eroded washes into the rivers with each winter's rain, 'pouring off the hills in great chocolate torrents' as the excavator of Jarmo described, providing the source of the alluvium which has extended the southern plain of Iraq by a hundred miles since the fourth millennium BC. So even before the rise of the first cities in the plain, mankind was changing the balance with nature forever, as it continues to do today. And no doubt it was the pressure on a growing population to open up

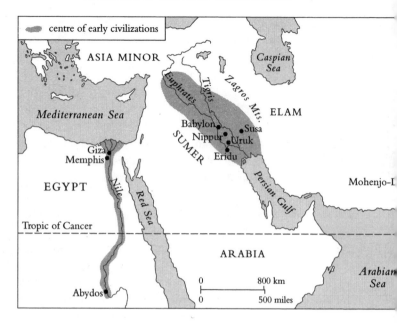

Above: The first civilizations. All the early civilizations of the Old World arose on rivers, in similar climatic conditions, and around the same latitude. Iraq's contacts with Egypt, the Iranian plateau and the Indus went back deep into prehistory; China, it seems, was a completely original growth.

Right: Nippur, the sacred city of Sumer. Details of the walls, gates and other named features come from a remarkable map of around 1300 BC. In the first millennium AD the west mound was the heart of the city.

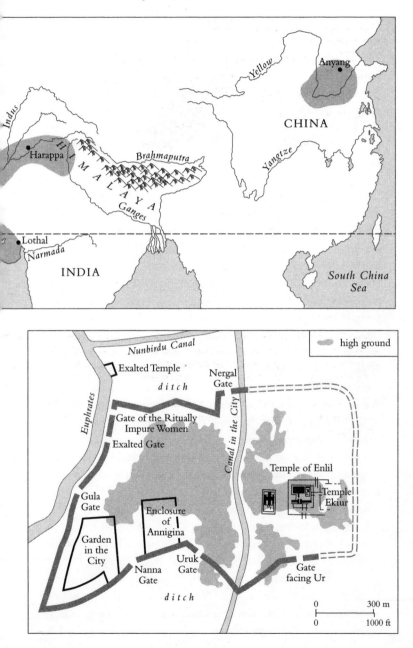

new land which led large groups of people for the first time into the deep south.

When exactly did people first settle the plain? There must have been hunter-gatherers moving across it since prehistory, as nomadic herders still do in our own time. But they have left no mark in the archaeological record, save for an intriguing but isolated Palaeolithic site near the most ancient cult shrine of the south at Eridu. But ten miles north of Warka, possibly from as early as 5000 BC, comes an enigmatic settlement which may give a clue. Only 300 feet across, this was the home of perhaps three family groups. They made pottery, fished with nets and baked clay weights; they had stone tools, grinding stones and a quern; they fashioned clay figurines of the mother goddess like those in common use in later times. Their houses perhaps were of mud and reed. The growth of such communities can be traced over the next millennium by their distinctive pottery, which is known as Ubaid after one of the important early sites. These were perhaps the first permanent people of the south. They were not Sumerian, that is, they did not speak the language we call Sumerian, for the early place names of Sumer – Ur, Eridu, Uruk, Nippur – are not from that language. Presumably then it was the Ubaid people who first named the southern landscape; the Sumerian speakers, it is assumed, came into the plain from the south-east around 4000 BC, into an already existing culture. But who the Sumerians were is still one of archaeology's great mysteries. Their language has no known affinities with any language, living or dead. But new discoveries concerning Elamite, the ancient language of Persia (see pages 55–7), may hold the key to Sumerian origins.

Living links with that deep past still survive which help us to imagine these early steps towards civilization. The permanent settlements of the Ubaid people were perhaps very similar to traditional mudbrick villages still to be seen in the plain only twenty or thirty years ago. Near the mound of ancient Shurrupak, in the middle of Sumer, for example, is a village abandoned in the 1960s when its canal dried up. It had a population of 200, who lived in mud and reed huts. Each family group had an enclosure wall of sun-dried mud protecting their house, a sleeping platform, corral, grain silo, and bread oven. The village still had an old female traditional religious specialist who composed verses, incantations and spells, and acted as midwife. In architecture, customs and language, theirs was an archaic world harking back to long before Islam. In the deep south of the plain, today's Marsh Arab settlements must also look much as the Ubaidian and Sumerian settlements once did, scattered along the alluvium: built on man-made islands in the freshwater lagoons where they live by fishing, cutting the reed beds, and cultivating the rich soil along the shores. Their elaborate reed houses, some up to 100 feet long, and their slim and elegant boats sealed with natural bitumen, are still built in the same fashion as was depicted 5000 years ago in Sumerian art. Here it was still possible, at least up to the Gulf War and its aftermath, to enter into a world which recalls the early myths. It is a world of small artificial islands each built on reed piles, with a reed house, barn, *mudhif*, clay kiln and bread oven, and a painted boat. Here a single family might live with their animals, their cows and water buffalo (which were first introduced from India in the third millennium BC). Such islands are worlds in miniature – living symbols of the way the people of southern Iraq have patiently laboured for millennia to create land out of water and life and civilization out of the plain and the swamp under that vast and unremitting sky.

So even today in the southern plain the visitor can find clues to the different lives lived by prehistoric societies on the threshold of the city age. There are the mudbrick villages of the sedentary cultivators and herders. There is too the purely nomadic life still followed by the Bedouin, moving their black tented camps up and down the plain from summer to winter pasture. And then the Marsh Arabs constitute a mixture of the two. In such a fluid world, the opportunities of permanent settlements are obvious. By exchanging grains and vegetables for the produce of the marsh dwellers or the Bedouin herders, it would be possible to build up a surplus and to deal long distance for precious metals and luxuries. Along with the social and economic causes of urbanization then, we should not overlook human ambition. The Sumerians had a deeply ingrained drive for worldly success.

Religion, too, must have played its part. When they emerge, the cities of Sumer centre on shrines of the deities of the plain, gods of wind, air and sky, of the grape vine, the grain, and fertility; shrines for the herders, the cattlefolk, the fisherpeople. They were often situated in border regions. The goddess of childbirth at Kesh was 'at the top of the plain'; Nippur, the city of the wind god Enlil, was on the northern edge of Sumer; Enki of Eridu, lord of the fresh water, was at the bottom on the marshes; Sin the Moon God was at Ur on the sea. These were liminal places where the fishermen or the herders of the grasslands could exchange with the settled cultivators. And even today, out in the desert the traveller will come across little Islamic shrines of plastered brick surrounded by heaps of gear – bikes, ploughs, tools, transistor radios – left for safekeeping by nomads or seasonal shepherds. Perhaps in ancient times, such favourable meeting places grew bigger, becoming permanent settlements for the storing of treasure, goods and produce, and eventually places of exchange. Perhaps at the root of the Mesopotamian city, for good practical reasons, was the shrine.

THE FIRST CITIES

Not long before 3000 BC, the first true cities in the world arose in Mesopotamia. Later Sumerian written tradition names the first place in Sumer, the earliest shrine: Eridu. Lost to the world for over two thousand years, Eridu was identified in 1853 by John Taylor, the British Vice-Consul in Basra who also did pioneering archaeological work at Ur, the city of Abraham. Twelve miles out into the desert beyond Ur, the mound of Eridu was called by the local nomads Abu Shahrein, 'Father of the Two Crescent Moons.' This may allude to the motif found on its walls (Eridu had a 'New Moon Quay') though just conceivably may recall the ancient cult at nearby Ur, a memory of which survived among the local Arabs as 'Moon City.'

Eridu is lonely, windswept and abandoned today; it had a brief strange afterlife as an anti-aircraft gun post in the war with Iran. But it was one of the most famous places in the history of Mesopotamia. The Sumerians believed that it was the site of the mound of creation, the first land which rose from the primal sea at the beginning of time. They thought that kingship – that is political society – first came down to earth here. Their myths also describe how the arts of civilization were initially possessed by Eridu before any other city. It originally stood at the edge of a great sea of fresh water stretching out to the south, the Apsu, from which apparently comes our word 'abyss.' The great temple here, the most ancient shrine in Sumer, was also named Apsu. This was the dwelling place of Enki, the archaic god of the waters, the god of wisdom, named after that primeval ocean of sweet water out of which all human life and all natural life came, as they believed. Indeed, at least as late as the tenth century AD there were still old sects in the southern marshes and coasts who worshipped the waters and whose myths and cosmologies incorporated Sumerian myths. Here too in a walled garden stood the sacred Kiskanu tree, 'which gleamed like lapis lazuli', perhaps the prototype of the Tree of Life in the Biblical garden of Eden.

Eridu had to wait till 1949 before there was a full-scale excavation deep into the mound below the platform of the temple ziggurat built in 2000 BC by the kings of nearby Ur. When the archaeologists dug into the temple hill they uncovered nineteen levels below the ziggurat, going back to the founding of the shrine around 5000 BC. At the bottom was a little sand mound surrounded by a reed fence with a tiny chapel, marking the site of the mythical mound of creation. If anywhere, then, here is the origin of the Biblical story of the garden of Eden. For what the Bible calls paradise, Eden, was simply the Sumerian word *Edin*, the wild, uncultivated grassland of the south, the natural landscape which lay outside the artificial landscape of the city. And picking over the debris of paradise, it is hard not to see the psychological truth of the Bible story: that the very beginning of our ascent to civilization was also the fall, when we tasted the fateful fruit of the tree of knowledge: the means by which we would become masters of the earth and yet eventually gain the power to destroy it and ourselves.

Such speculations become all the more pointed when we look at the layers of Eridu which superseded the early Ubaidian village with its primitive mud and reed shrine. For around 4000 BC a dramatic change came over the hill. Massive ceremonial buildings were constructed, a huge shrine in a monumental style of architecture. Grand tombs for an élite suggest class divisions were now in existence. Gold and metal-working and imported luxuries hint that the élite now controlled Eridu's surplus wealth. Several thousand people now lived around the hill. Perhaps in these clues we can see the very moment when 'kingship came down to earth' and political power fell into the hands of the few.

The Eridu myths then perhaps are reflections of a real historical process, from the creation of organized communities in the south of the plain, to the arrival of the temple, the city, and kingship. These, in sum, were the key arts of civilization which Sumerian myth believed originated in Eridu and were passed on by the gods to future ages from Eridu to the first true city on earth, Uruk.

To get to Uruk from Eridu today, you cross southern Iraq, skirting Ur and Nasiriyah, names familiar now after the war of 2003. You cross the Euphrates beyond Samawa, then head south-east into the desert, where you enter a lunar landscape, a wasteland swept by gales of sand. Immense mounds loom out of the haze in a furnace heat. It can be 135° Fahrenheit out here in the summer. Finally you come to a city gate, still visible after nearly five thousand years, its approach silted with a deep tide of pottery and bones. This is where William Loftus stood in 1849.

Still 50 feet high, the line of eroded walls curves round to the horizon. The centre of the city is dominated by the ruins of a great stepped tower, a ziggurat on which once stood the temple of the city's goddess, Inanna, whom we know as Ishtar. The first city may have begun as a religious centre, perhaps a shrine for the herders of the plain, in the quarter known as Kullaba, the sky god's shrine. The goddess's sanctuary came later. From the top of the ziggurat you can see what is left of the rich landscape of Sumer. Once fertile fields criss-crossed by canals, lined with palm groves, the territory of Uruk is now parched, wind-blown desert. To the north-east, beyond a dried bed of the Euphrates, is a huge cone-shaped tomb from the Persian period. All over the desert are the signs of human habitation: ruined irrigation canals, broken pottery, twisted slag. Beyond are the tell-tale mounds of ancient cities, some of which the ancients believed had existed even before the Flood. On the horizon, lit by the setting sun, you can just make out the mound of Larsa. Further out are Umma, one of the oldest cities in Sumer, and Tel Jidr, which survived into the Middle Ages. Out of sight to the north across huge sand dunes is Shurrupak, home town of the Sumerian Noah. There are, surely, few more extraordinary landscapes in the world.

From the top of the goddess's ziggurat the full extent of Uruk becomes apparent, with its walled circuit of more than six miles. There were two settlements here before 4000 BC, a sizeable city during the next millennium; but modern archaeology has shown that the walls were built at the end of a period of remarkable expansion when Uruk increased four times in size in just a few generations from about 3000 to 2700 BC. Presumably then, tens of thousands of people were moving in from the countryside to this new city life. There are distant parallels for this kind of large-scale change from rural to urban life. In China between 1100 and 1250 AD, southern cities like Hangchow increased five times in population, fed by a revolution in agriculture. In England during the industrial revolution, the population increased more than four times in a single century before 1800. In some parts of medieval Europe, too, between 1100 and 1300, a tenfold population increase occurred in regions where new land could be opened up through land reclamation and irrigation. In Europe this seems to have gone hand-in-hand with a lowering of the marriage age, which has the effect of accelerating the birth rate by lessening the gap between generations.

Bearing such ideas in mind we can see how a combination of similar factors could have worked in the early third millennium BC. Improved irrigation and land reclamation created more land; intensive cultivation produced more food; larger walled settlements brought more security; more land, more food and better security encouraged people to leave the countryside and to live in the cities, moving from the uplands into the southern plain. The inexorable pull of the cities' markets with their necessities and luxuries must have made them additionally attractive, as cities have been throughout history. Then, once powerful rulers were able to impose their control, whether kings, priesthoods or noble families (or a combination of all three), they were no doubt able to place heavy burdens on the poorer peasantry; for some among the masses in old Sumer, the 'urban miracle' may have been as grim as it was in the nineteenth-century industrial city. For the answers to many of these questions we are still in the dark, not least about the social and power structures which brought about this great historical change, and in particular in the origins of kingship. But like their nineteenth-century successors they were in no doubt as to the greatness of their achievement: 'Look at the walls of Uruk, gleaming like burnished bronze; inspect its inner wall, the like of which no man can equal! Go up on the wall of Uruk and walk around: examine its foundation, look at its brickwork – even the inner core is kiln-fired brick. Didn't the Seven Sages themselves lay out its plans?' [*Epic of Gilgamesh*]

Another Sumerian poem, the story of Etana, gives us an imagined bird's-eye view of such cities, and conveys something of their dizzying effect on the imagination of those early generations who lived through this first urban miracle. Looking down on the plain from miles up, on the brown desert and the blue sea, on the warrens of houses, and on their populations with 'the business of the country ceaselessly buzzing like a myriad insects,' Etana is lost in admiration at humankind's ability to reshape its environment.

26

In the peak period of the third millennium BC there were some forty cities in Sumer and Akkad, which together made up the Babylonian plain, mainly independent city states. They were densely settled. A big city state like Lagash had 36,000 male adults, Uruk perhaps the same. They were closely organized and controlled. In Nippur at a later period, there were 200 subsidiary villages in its territory, clustered around five main canals and sixty lesser ones, joined by a web of countless small irrigation ditches, all of which were subject to rules, duties and control, a constant source of litigation!

As for the physical make-up of the city itself, according to the Epic of Gilgamesh, Uruk was one-third built up, one-third gardens, one-third temple property. Excavated streets in Ur and Nippur look just like the warrens of houses still visible in old Irbil, Kirkuk, Tel Afar, or at the sacred city of Najaf. In today's Irbil the 4000 people who still live inside the now decaying citadel belong to three wards, one to each gate; each has a small shrine, bath and souk; each too had its scribe or writer. These arrangements are an exact echo of ancient Ur or Nippur. The design of houses in the ancient cities was identical to that used up till the advent of air conditioning, with central courtyards, windcatchers, and serdabs (sunken rooms) to keep the ferocious summer heat at bay. The pattern of streets also served to create shadow and allow the breeze to blow through: only in the last thirty years has this older Iraq disappeared.

At the centre of the ancient city was the temple, as the mosque is today, and they were no doubt run in the same manner as now. In Nippur for example in 2000 BC, the Ur-Meme family administered the Inanna temple for generations. Just so, in Irbil today, the Al-Mulla family have run the main mosque for the last 600 years, producing distinguished poets, astronomers and scholars. In Baghdad the Gailani family have administered the greatest of the city's shrines since the twelfth century, and in many ways it resembles the temples of old, with its philanthropic role in the community, its library, its great kitchen and hostels, and its wide landholdings across the Diyala plain. The ancient city then has its lineal descendant in the medieval – and even in some cases, the modern – Islamic city.

But there is another way in which the Mesopotamian city resembles its modern counterpart: it was parasitical of the soil and the environment. The plain around Uruk was once big wheat country with grain yields as high as the Mid-West and Canada; today it is salt-encrusted and barren as far as the eye can see. The need for more land and for more intensive cultivation to feed an ever-growing population eventually devastated the landscape. We know now that civilization inevitably destroys the environment, but they discovered it here for the first time. The most telling proof of this is that there is virtually no continuity in land use between the great periods of Mesopotamian history, between the ancients, the Hellenistic and Sassanian, the Islamic and the modern. Improved irrigation and fertilization, better use of fallow periods, and especially the cutting of huge new dykes by the Sassanians and the Arabs all enabled some landscapes to regenerate and live on. But essentially each of these great epochs had to open up new areas for cultivation, leaving the old land, now exhausted, to return to desert.

So it is a salutary experience today to walk the weathered gullies of 'wide-wayed Uruk,' littered with testimony to the long ascent of man, if such it is. Here were enormous temples as big as cathedrals, their façades decorated with blue glazed tiles, just as can be seen today on the mosques of Iraq. Still visible are the platforms of the vast shrines rebuilt in traditional Babylonian style in the third century BC under the Greek successors of Alexander the Great, when Uruk was still rich and populous, and perhaps still a major centre of pilgrimage. At that time the cities of Old Sumer still preserved their own civil customs and organization and were still built in the old way, still worshipping the old gods. As late as the Christian period there was some life left in the old place. In the south-east quarter of the city centre is a small temple to a local god Gareus, dedicated in November 110 AD by a guild of Greek-speaking locals from near Mosul: probably merchants who engaged in the old trade down the Gulf and beyond, to

Bahrain and the Indus. On the back wall is the same fish-tailed sea goddess which can be seen in shrines in Gujerat and the Gulf of Cambay, where Iraqi merchants still trade today.

With the ups and downs of any living organism, the city of Uruk and its institutions lasted through to about 300 AD. A small settlement outside the walls survived till the Arab conquest. Indeed, even in the eighth century the local Christian bishop still called himself 'Bishop of Uruk and Kaskar.' But by then it was dead, after a life of over five thousand years.

THE MOTHER OF INVENTION

Amid this vast rubbish tip of human history are clues to the genius of these first city builders. Everywhere are fragments of pottery: wheel-turned pottery, with a beautiful greenish colour and fine black geometric patterns. The wheel is found here in Sumer for the first time in history, along with so many of the great inventions we still live our lives by today. Here was the first astronomy, the first literature, the first law, the first school, the first map of the world. Here they first thought of dividing time and space in multiples of sixty, so that even now whenever we look at a watch we are still in their debt.

The greatest of all Sumerian inventions however was writing. Writing is first found in the world in Uruk, maybe invented in this city by some unknown genius, not long before 3000 BC. Most of the writing found on Iraqi sites, more than ninety-five per cent of it in fact, is economic texts: facts and figures, bills, accounts, inventories, measures of dates or barley, parcels of land down to every rod, pole or perch. Contrast that with the earliest Sanskrit (religious texts) or the Chinese oracle bones (shamanistic divination) and you have the clearest possible indicator of the different character of these civilizations right from the outset. Here in Mesopotamia is the birth of economic man whose relations are bound by secular law: *homo oeconomicus*, the root idea of the modern west.

Nevertheless, perhaps the most enduring legacy of

Mesopotamian culture is its imaginative literature, and especially its myths. Iraqis have always been great story-tellers, going back long before the Thousand and One Nights to the world's first literature in Sumerian, and to the Epic of Gilgamesh. Gilgamesh was almost certainly a real person; perhaps, as later legend said, the King of Uruk who built the walls around 2700 BC. With him would be associated the Sumerian tale of the Flood and the great ark, which many centuries later appeared in the Bible and is known today right across the world. Gilgamesh's last adventure was his futile quest for everlasting life, accompanied by his ever faithful friend Enkidu, the 'wild man' alter ego of the 'civilized' city man. It is the model for all searches, from the Odyssey to the Holy Grail and Indiana Jones. His stories were copied, translated and told in the Near East right down to Greek times. Some motifs crept into the Homeric epics in the Aegean world in the eighth century BC. They survived in versions overlaid with Jewish and Hellenistic elements in the first centuries AD. Then they reappear with Muslim colouring in Islamic times in the Thousand and One Nights, the tales of Aladdin and Sindbad, where Buluqiya's search for everlasting life and the Tree of Paradise is an unmistakable echo of Gilgamesh. In the eighth century AD his tale was still remembered in the old southern heartland in Kaskar, close to the now dead city whose walls he may have built; when the local Nestorian bishop in a religious handbook mentioned him among the kings who ruled after the Flood, 'in whose days Abraham was born in Ur of the Chaldees.' Doubtless the bishop heard the tale at his mother's knee, for similar stories have survived even till now in Iraq.

The story of Gilgamesh also brings us to one of the characteristic qualities of Mesopotamian civilization from the earliest times till today: its pessimism. For over three thousand years, from ancient times to the golden age of Islam, its literature, proverbs and religious texts all reveal the same sensibility, so different from the optimistic quality of Egyptian civilization, or the ethical confidence of classical China. It is there in the recension of Gilgamesh done by the Uruk master scribe Sinleqiuninni in around 1300 BC, in the most famous lines of ancient Babylonian literature:

> Gilgamesh, what you seek you will never find. For when the Gods created Man they let death be his lot, eternal life they withheld. Let your every day be full of joy, love the child that holds your hand, let your wife delight in your embrace, for these alone are the concerns of humanity.

THE FALL OF SUMER

Given their collective dependence on the Euphrates system for irrigation, it was in the interests of all the city states of the south of Iraq to co-operate despite their differences. But internecine warfare is the constant theme of the first age of cities, the third millennium BC. In this there could hardly be a greater contrast with Egypt, which united early and generally stayed united. The rivalry between city states was often bitter, as in the long-running feud between Umma and Girsu over the control of their branch of the Euphrates (2500–2300 BC). The overlordship of the dynasty of Akkad (2300–2150 BC), dominating the north of the plain, was another time of conflict. The last heyday of an independent south took place between 2100 and 2000 BC under the leadership of the city of Ur. Founded by a general, Ur Nammu, the Third Dynasty of Ur harked back to an ancient and glorious Sumerian past. Great ziggurats were built at the old cult shrines of Sumer – Uruk, Eridu, Ur, Larsa and Nippur; their temples were beautified and embellished with treasures. Ur Nammu and his kinsmen sponsored the copying of literature about the heroes of the Old Sumerian heartland, the Kings of Uruk, and especially Gilgamesh, with whom they claimed kinship. In his forty-eight years' reign, Shulgi of Ur initiated massive and costly administrative reforms including the revival of an archaic custom of tribute by the nineteen cities of Sumer to the 'national' shrine at Nippur, where vast numbers of animals and supplies were brought each month to a central depot for sacrifice at the temples. That this enormous expenditure contributed to the dynasty's economic troubles seems likely. The climate of the plain seems now to have been going through a long, dry spell; much agricultural land had gone out of use, and economic documents show administrators shifting from wheat to the more salt-resistant barley to combat salinization. Worse, the perennial raids on the plain from nomadic outsiders grew more and more threatening. Shulgi's successor Shu-sin built and garrisoned a 'Martu wall' in the north-west to keep out one group of invaders from Syria. The roof finally fell in on his successor, Ibbi Sin. There is evidence that much land by now had been abandoned through salinization. The population could not be fed: prices hit the ceiling with a sixtyfold increase in grain. International trade, on which Sumer had always depended for its raw materials, broke down, and soon government communications started to fail. Panic-stricken messages survive between the king and his agents as his enemies closed in. Gloomy oracles prophesied the worst, and the worst duly arrived. It was the perennial problem of Iraqi history – how to hold the rich and populous plain, with no natural boundaries, against the many outside enemies covetous of its wealth: a drama still being played out in the early twenty-first century.

The end of the Third Dynasty of Ur was one of the greatest events in the history of Sumer. Around 2000 BC the land was devastated by a coalition of its enemies, Elamites from what is now Iran, and their nomadic allies from the desert. All the main cities of Sumer were sacked, their temples destroyed, their treasures plundered, and their populations killed, enslaved or forced to flee. Finally Ur itself was wrecked and burned, and Ibbi Sin carried off to Elam as a prisoner. These terrible events left an indelible mark on the psyche of the culture. Several lamentations survive describing in graphic detail the destruction of Sumer and its cities:

Ur is destroyed, bitter is its lament. The country's blood now fills its holes like hot bronze in a mould. Bodies dissolve like fat in the sun.

Our temple is destroyed, the gods have abandoned us, like migrating birds. Smoke lies on our city like a shroud.

These laments were performed every year in temple festivals in the south right down to the Hellenistic Greek age; they were recited too whenever a temple was rebuilt after destruction in war or peace, as if forever to remind the people of the fragility of civilization. The lament itself was an ancient form in Sumerian culture and the city laments are only part of a huge number of compositions (called *ersemma* or *balag*) which survive from temple archives, confirming our impression of a uniquely pessimistic vision of history and human destiny: indeed, as we shall see, it is difficult not to associate this sensibility with the later culture of Shiism which arose in the same fertile soil of southern Iraq.

FROM THE ANCIENT WORLD TO ISLAM

The urban civilization of southern Iraq was restored after the destruction of 2000 BC, its cities and temples rebuilt. Indeed, through many destructions it proved uniquely long-lasting and durable. In the second and first millennia BC, Mesopotamia was ruled in turn by Babylonians, Kassites, Hittites, Assyrians, Nebuchadnezzar's Neo-Babylonians, Persians, Greeks, Parthians, and subsequently by Sassanian Persians in the period before the Arab conquest. Most of these dynasties were foreign, but the culture remained Mesopotamian, in custom, organization and in the language of the root population, whose Arabic today is descended from the Aramaic spoken across the Near East in early Christian times, which in its turn comes from the Semitic Akkadian already spoken throughout Babylonia by 2000 BC. (Sumerian by then it seems was already a dead language, though still used for recording literary and liturgical texts in Greek times). Right down to the third century BC the great temples in the south retained their own cults and organization, and were rebuilt in the ancient local tradition. But the world was changing fast. The Greek conquest of the Near East under Alexander opened up the region to new currents of thought. Iraq as always was a crossroads where East and West met, and the international culture of Hellenism inaugurated an era of tremendous speculation about culture, civilization and history, and about God. During the next centuries, the Fertile Crescent gave birth to new universal religions, all of which could draw inspiration from the diverse traditions and contacts stirred up by the Greek epoch and the mixing of Persian, Arab, Jewish and Greek religion and culture which it had brought about. By the fourth century AD Christianity and Manichaeism were both ambitious to be world religions. But as it turned out, the most successful crystal-lization of change in the Middle East was Islam. Like the others, Islam drew on Jewish, Christian and Zoroastrian elements, but with its radical and democratic message, and its use of the Arabic language, it transformed the ancient cultures of the Near East.

In the seventh century AD Arab armies bearing the new faith of Islam swept into Mesopotamia, overcoming the armies of the Sassanian Persian Empire which was now in decline. Like most invaders in history, they were a small minority. The majority of the population of Iraq adopted Islam during the next four hundred years, but they did not follow the Sunni tradition of their Arab conquerors. After the Arab conquest in the south of Iraq, old Sumer, Islam took on a distinctive local form which remained in touch with ancient roots: Shiism. The mass of the people of Iraq, the poor farmers of the south who were descendants of the Aramaic-speaking population of pre-Islamic Mesopotamia, never forsook their ancient forms of worship even though their faith now focused on the seventh-century martyrdoms of Hussayn and Ali, whom they believe to be the true inheritors of the Prophet's spiritual authority. This ancient split between Sunni and Shia is still at the heart of the Islamic world today. In the sacred city of Kerbala, the Shiites carried the ancient Sumerian tradition of lamentation close to their hearts, as no other faith has done. And so it had been for thousands of years before Islam. Many of the customs of the Shia seem to hark back to an earlier Iraqi past: their forms of worship, purification rituals, marriage contract, the organization of the priesthood, and their burial customs. Shia lamentations, especially the female form, also offer close parallels with the ancient world. These remarkable traditions are perhaps a survival of the most deep-rooted Mesopotamian religious experience. Even the physical appearance of the great Shiite mosques of Hussayn and Abbas at Kerbala and Ali at Najaf recalls the buildings of old Sumer. Though reconstructed many times in Persian style by Iranian benefactors, the elaborate mosaics and geometrical designs on their façades still reproduce patterns like those which had adorned the shrines of Uruk, Ubaid and Eridu; 'True temples,' as the Sumerian hymns said, 'shining like rainbows in the bright sun.'

THE WORLD OF EARLY ISLAM

In the first centuries of Muslim Arab rule, Iraq was very prosperous. Two fascinating snapshots of Mesopotamia survive from the tenth century, one by Ibn Serabh (*c*.900) the other in a Persian geography of 982. Both portray its fertility and its thriving urban life, 'the abode of scholars and merchants … with running waters and flourishing countryside.' One of the prosperous towns of that time was the old sacred city of Mesopotamia, Nippur. In the centuries after the Islamic conquest a mixed society arose here in a town as multicultural as any big city in the USA today, a far cry from the conventional view of Islam we hold in the West. In the maze of mudbrick streets there was a thriving Jewish community with its own scribal school. The Talmud, the greatest collection of Hebrew custom, was written in southern Iraqi towns like Nippur during the first millennium AD, in a time of dynamic interplay between Jewish and Islamic culture. In addition to the Friday mosque, there was a Nestorian Christian Church here with a bishop; Christians were still probably in the majority in the tenth century. There were Mandaeans and Manichaeans (their prophet Mani was born near Ctesiphon, raised in the marshes, and went on to found a world religion which spread from Iraq across Asia as far as China).

But whatever community you belonged to, you still relied on the old Babylonian folklore of planets, stars and demons. Even today magical incantation bowls are turned up after heavy rain in the wadis of the western quarter of the old city of Nippur, inscribed in Hebrew, Syriac, Mandaic and in the Aramaic used by the followers of Mani. These give us an intriguing insight into the continuing world of old Babylonian magic in the years leading up to and after the Islamic conquest. Their function was quite simple. If you had a problem you went to see the sorcerer who lived in your quarter of the city and he would draw up a spell for you, inscribing the spell in a spiral inside the bowl. The spell might, for example, ask the demoness Lilith (an ancient Babylonian spirit) to 'get out of our lives, leave my wife alone, leave my family alone, my sheep, my cattle, my fields, depart from us.' The sorcerer would also paint a picture of the demon in the centre of the bowl. Some of them were bug-like creatures, with their feet shackled to keep them down, others were depicted with ziggurats as heads, as if the ruined towers still carried a numinous power. You then took the bowl home and sealed it inside the wall or the threshold of your house, placed upside down so that the demon would be trapped inside. These bowls chart the final decline of the ancient Babylonian gods, now mere devils daubed on incantation bowls in spells for the urban poor. Here are Bel and Nergal; Greek deities too, such as Zeus, Hermes and Apollo, and Iranian spirits from the period of Sassanian rule in Iraq. Such then was the sad end of Inanna 'great goddess of the universe', who appears as the jinn Nanna on the bowls. In these ways spirit worlds change and metamorphose over time. Amazingly some of those old beliefs, especially the incantation magic, survived among the poor people of Iraq – Jewish, Christian and Muslim – right up to our own time: specialists in folk religion were still to be found in the southern countryside even in the 1960s, wise men or 'openers' with their books of charms.

In the ninth century, in the south of Iraq, this vibrant mix of

Arab and Persian culture, Jewish, Christian and Muslim religion, gave birth to a new mystical movement and some of the world's supreme religious poets, the Sufis. By this time Baghdad and the cities of Iraq were at the centre of the Islamic world. Industrial and trading cities like Kufa and Basra were hotbeds of intellectual and religious ferment, their trade routes with India and Central Asia, Egypt and the Mediterranean a constant vehicle for ideas and artefacts. Many of the early Sufis from Baghdad and Basra drew on such diverse inspiration. The great mystic and martyr al-Hallaj knew Christian and Greek gnosis and had visited India, where he perhaps encountered the *Upanishads* and the *Bhagavad Gita*. Another great Sufi was born at the old sacred city of Nippur: al Niffari, the 'Man of Visions.' Through the 950s and 960s, like Hallaj, Niffari wandered in many lands, including Egypt, though always returning to the south, to Basra, Nil and Nippur; scribbling his revelations in notebooks, 'words committed to him by gift and favour of God.' Not surprisingly, perhaps, in a place of such immemorial traditions – in the shadow of the ruined ziggurat of Ur Nammu – Niffari's visions seem to speak to us still in the haunting voice of Old Sumer. 'I saw fear holding sway over hope, and riches turn to dust, I saw poverty as the enemy, I saw this world to be a delusion and heaven to be a deception, I saw every created thing, and it fled from me and I was left here alone.'

Most of the communities in early Islamic Mesopotamia survived into modern times. When Nippur finally died in the fourteenth century, the Mandaean community migrated to the deep marshes, to Amara and Suk-esh-Shuyukh and the thirty other villages recorded by early European travellers. There they lived until the twentieth century, when many moved to Baghdad to pursue their traditional craft of gold and metal working. They are still there. Protected by the Koran, along with Jews and Christians, as 'people of the book,' the Mandaeans are an astonishing survival of ancient Mesopotamian religious traditions, but they also put us in touch with the baptismal culture out of which Christianity arose. Originating in Palestine, like Jesus they called themselves followers of John the Baptist: *mandayye* or *nasorayya*. (Was Jesus *Nazoraios*, as Matthew calls him, then really not of Nazareth at all, but a 'Nasorayan', a baptist 'gnostic' or 'observer'?)

The Mandaean wedding ceremonies are accompanied by full immersion in the Tigris, which in commemoration they still call the Jordan. The ritual takes place in Mandaic, a dialect of the Aramaic which Jesus spoke. Other customs reflect their near 2000-year residence in Babylonia. When the bishop consecrates a new priest, he must undergo an ordeal in the dark blue tent, the colour of the evil eye: staying awake for seven days and seven nights just as Gilgamesh was required to do in his own failed initiation into the nether world. The Mandaeans are a reminder of how pluralism and tolerance are essential qualities of civilization, and a reminder too, of how ordinary Iraqi people, despite the catastrophes of their history, have down the years tenaciously preserved some of their most ancient traditions. 'Life is victorious,' says the Mandaean marriage service, and indeed, what if a man gain the whole world and lose his soul?

BAGHDAD: 'FIRST CITY OF THE WORLD'

Baghdad itself had been founded on the west bank of the Tigris by the Arab conquerors of Iraq in the eighth century, one of the last of the great Mesopotamian planned cities. Where Babylon had been a huge rhomboid, Borsippa a square, and Akkad a triangle, the core of Abbasid Baghdad was a vast circle two miles across with zones for trades, crafts, industry and shops spreading out from the royal mosque in the middle. Surrounded by a tracery of canals in the suburbs, this was a city of waterways like Venice. It became the greatest cultural centre in the world: 'a city of scholars and great riches,' said the Persian geographer of 982, 'the most prosperous town in the world, the haunt of merchants, thronging with people.' Little survives of that time today. Successive destructions of Baghdad have virtually erased all trace, save for the old cemetery and the wind-blown memorial to Hallaj. The medieval walled city stood on the east bank, where

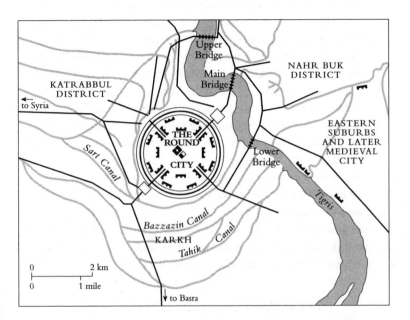

Baghdad c.800–1000 AD. The Round City was surrounded by suburbs for crafts and trades: the hundreds of booksellers, for example, were to be found between the Sart and Bazzazin canals.

fragments of walls and gates and some medieval buildings still stand: chief among them is the mosque of the city's patron saint, Abd al-Gailani, still a great centre for pilgrimage. It was built at a time when colleges and philanthropic institutions were being created throughout Islam, before the universities of the West, before Oxford, the Sorbonne and Bologna: a grand college-cum-shrine with its kitchens and ancillary buildings in the old style of religious institutions of Mesopotamia. The civilized atmosphere of its courtyards brings to mind the great scholars of the past who learned and taught here, scholars who translated the sacred books of the Jews and Christians, 'so that,' as they said, 'we might better understand the decisions of God.' Medieval Baghdad was renowned for such open-minded curiosity. Think of al-Nadim, for example, son of one of the 800 humanist booksellers in tenth-century Baghdad, who attempted to write 'a catalogue of the books of all peoples, Arab or foreign, written in Arabic, dealing with the various sciences, with accounts of those who composed them.' There was al-Masudi, the historian who interviewed Christians, Zoroastrians, Jews, Greeks and even Hindus for his *Historical Annals*, and whose researches led him from Turkey to the Deccan in India. And what of Al-Razi, the great physician who revolutionized Arab medicine, and who, by-the-by, denied the truth of *any* prophet? 'Humane learning,' wrote one of the best teachers here, Abd al-Latif, 'leaves an aura, like a ray of bright light shining on those who come after.'

Inside Gailani's shrine the visitor is reminded once again of the old customs of Mesopotamian worship, in the glittering holy of holies shimmering with mirrors and prisms, whose magnificence distantly reflects something still of the old pre-Islamic world. Saint, poet and mystic, Gailani was founder of one of the great Sufi orders, the Qadiriya, and to pause for thought in his shrine is to feel what a dynamic force Iraqi Islam – Shia and Sunni – has been through history. The 'fundamentalist' Shiism sponsored by Khomeini and the ayatollahs of Iran since the revolution of 1979 may be a very different thing from the traditional Islam of the medieval humanists, let alone the visionary masters like Ibn Arabi or Suhrawardi, but now at the start of the twenty-first century, however much the rich and complacent West may wish it otherwise, Islam is once again a great power in the world, a beacon for the dispossessed peoples of Asia and Africa. It is an ideal for which people still live and die precisely because, in the battle now being fought all over the world between tradition and modernity, it offers an alternative to the modern secular values of the West.

THE SACK OF BAGHDAD

From the time of Harun al Rashid (763–809 AD) till the eleventh century, Baghdad was one of the three greatest cities in the world, along with Constantinople and Xian in China. And like them it was one of the great transmitters by which the cultural legacy of the ancients was passed on to the medieval and modern world. The scholarship of the medieval city was helped in no small measure by paper, which was introduced from China in the mid-eighth century, enabling the mass production of books at a low cost. This was a world of correspondence, libraries and bookshops, a book culture. Baghdad was also the great intermediary in the meeting between Persian and Arabic culture which continues to bear fruit even today, and which in the past gave birth to some of the world's finest art, architecture, philosophy and literature. Also, and this is often forgotten in the West, much of the Greek scientific and philosophical legacy was passed on to us by Arab scholars; transformed in Baghdad by contact not only with Islam, but with the Mesopotamian legacy in astronomy and mathematics, and even gnostic and magical traditions of astrology and alchemy. In this extraordinary melting pot Christian, Greek and Iranian ideas in science, medicine and philosophy were reshaped through Arabic language, culture and scholarship. A transformation of the legacy of the ancients took place as potent and enriching as the later Renaissance in Europe.

But this tremendous adventure in pluralism and intellectual inquiry on which medieval Islamic culture embarked did not bear fruit in transforming the traditional societies of the Near East. Riven by internal struggles and social unrest, twelfth-century Baghdad was no longer the city it had been and Iraq was already in economic decline. Then there took place another of those cataclysms which have shifted the whole course of Mesopotamian history. Still looked upon as one of the greatest tragedies in the tragic history of Iraq, the long period of high culture in Baghdad was ended by the devastating Mongol attack of 1258, when the city was totally destroyed and its irrigation system ruined. The destruction of its libraries alone was an incalculable loss to the modern world. To mention but two, Nadim's autograph copy of his gigantic catalogue, the *Fihrist*, which at least survives in a partial copy; and Masudi's master work, the *Annals*, which was lost forever. In the aftermath, one of the survivors left this poignant note in a dog-eared and water-stained pocket commentary on the Koran which is still in the Gailani Library:

'I recovered this book from the River Tigris where it was thrown by the Mongols, Year of the Hejira 656. (1258 in the western calendar.) I am poor for the mercy of God, Mohammed Abdul Qadir from Mecca.' This is a testimony to enduring faith, not only in God but in the power of the written word to create civilization: one of the quintessential beliefs of Mesopotamian civilization from its very origins.

The Persian poet Saadi of Shiraz was in Abadan when he heard the news of the destruction of 'the first city of the world.' Looking out from his lodgings over the Tigris, in his mind's eye he saw the river running with blood. 'You ask me,' he wrote, 'about the sack of Baghdad? It was so horrible there are no words to describe it. I wish I had died earlier and not seen how the fools destroyed these treasures of knowledge and learning. I thought I understood the world, but this holocaust is so strange and pointless that I am struck dumb. The revolutions of time and its decisions have defeated reason and knowledge.'

INTO THE MODERN WORLD

The destruction of Baghdad in 1258 and the wrecking of the irrigation canals was a turning point in the history of the Middle East. 'There is no doubt,' said a Persian writer in grimly prophetic words, 'that even if for a thousand years to come, no evil befell Iraq, it will not be possible completely to bring back the land to the state it was before.' By the end of the sixteenth century, Iraq, the cradle of civilization, had sunk to the lowest level. The old cities of the south were dead, the land had returned to desert; even the new foundations of the Islamic period, Kufa and Wasit, had gone. Baghdad, although still active as a trading town, was a shadow of its former self, behind mudbrick walls in the quarter east of the Tigris, the city of the Caliphs now a vast ruin on the other side. In the south, only the port of Basra and the university and pilgrim city of Najaf still thrived. Four hundred years of Ottoman rule left the land plundered by a greedy military. The great events of the Renaissance, the Enlightenment, the discovery of the New World, passed it by. So, after all its great achievements, Iraq reached the modern age like a society stopped in time. Right up until the 1920s, its ancient towns looked no different from those of the third millennium BC. The extraordinary aerial photographic record made of Iraq in the 1920s by the British gives us a last image of this older Iraq, especially of the Shiite holy cities Samarra, Najaf, Kerbala and Khadimain. Here Najaf lies shimmering in the desert like a vision from the past; still entirely contained within its great mudbrick walls, outside which lie the baked Euphrates plain and the escarpment of the western desert. In the centre of the city the mosque of Ali looks for all the world as we might imagine the ancient temples of Uruk or Eridu. In close-up at the north-west corner of the shrine are winding alleys, souks, gabled houses with roof gardens and oriels, the warren of tenements still unlit by the morning sun. At this moment Najaf was still like an echo of the medieval world, with its craftsmen's guilds, its manuscript copiers, its bookshops and hostels, its holy men, teachers and pilgrims.

This spellbinding vision of an older world of Iraq survived till our own time, especially in the holy cities. Here the rich medieval Shia traditions of philosophy and jurisprudence were maintained with honour. Even in the 1960s the old culture of the booksellers and hand copiers was alive in Najaf. But all has been shattered now by the events of the last forty years, by a ruthless drive to modernize on the part of the Baathist regime, and especially by the Gulf wars of 1980–88 and 1991, the war in Kurdistan, and the invasion of 2003.

It was the discovery of oil, the second largest reserve in the world, which changed the course of Iraqi history. After the break-up of the Ottoman Empire the independence of the new state of Iraq became conditional on alliance with greater and more distant powers than had intervened in Mesopotamia in the past, still playing off the states and peoples of the region against each other in order to keep hold of the natural wealth of Mesopotamia. And so Iraq once again became a name on the world stage; the split between Shia and Sunni once again a matter of the greatest moment in Near Eastern history. Once more, in the 1980s, Iraq waged war against an enemy beyond the Zagros, the Persians; once more the land of the Two Rivers suffered foreign invasion.

THE DESTRUCTION OF SUMER, 1991

In 1991, a new war was fought in the south of Mesopotamia, in the desert where the first cities arose, another war over the natural resources of the earth, another war for civilization against barbarism. And once more, as in the ancient laments, we have seen smoke 'hanging like a shroud' over Sumer.

In the aftermath of the war of 1991 the Shiites of the south rose against their Sunni masters in Baghdad as they had done so often since the Middle Ages. Then Kerbala and Najaf, the sacred cities of Sumer, were sacked once more, and their shrines desecrated. Mosques and prayer halls were demolished, teachers executed or imprisoned, libraries destroyed, and manuscripts burned or looted.

After the uprising in 1991, the marshes of southern Iraq, home to the 5000-year-old culture of the Marsh Arabs, were ravaged and then partially drained; settlements were destroyed, a quarter of a million people displaced as the fire penetrated even the deep marshes. The long war fought by the government in Baghdad against the majority of its own people had finally reached the heart of the marshes, along with the devastated villages of Kurdistan and the brutalized and persecuted holy cities of the Shia. A systematic attempt to destroy the traditional native cultures of Iraq was reaching a climax; and this in the land where civilization had first defined its humane objectives, making law to moderate naked power, as the ancients said, 'to cause justice to prevail in the land, that the strong may not oppress the weak.' Ancient Babylonian scholars believed that history was not progress. Rather, they saw it as recurring cycles of human achievement which could be ended at any time by unforeseen disaster. Each time humanity must rebuild and start again: 'Once upon a time, Sumer, the great land of divine laws, had all that was needed for life. You, Sumer, set the ideals of civilization upon humankind, lofty ideals, robed in enduring light. Once upon a time ... when there was no fear, no terror.'

THE LEGACY OF IRAQ

The ancient civilization of Iraq was based on the city as a centre of economic and political life. It depended on international trade, on a diversified economy, and on thoroughgoing control of the environment. It used writing and written law to record and order transactions involving large numbers of its population. Theirs was a pluralistic society, as far as we can tell, multiracial from its earliest period. In tone, it was a pessimistic civilization, albeit a 'confident pessimism' as the Shia like to say: a vision deeply rooted in a harsh landscape where all that people worked for was often destroyed by war or nature, and still is.

The Mesopotamians conceived of civilization as separate from nature, set in an artificial environment of man's creation, which could insulate human society from the threats of primal nature (a contrast for example which lies at the heart of the Epic of Gilgamesh). And monotheism, the spiritual expression of Near Eastern culture, would see nature in the same light, the creator-god standing outside his creation, imparting its laws. Mesopotamian city civilization then represents a dramatic break with the cultural continuum of the prehistoric world which had lasted for tens of thousands of years, and which, as we shall see, would inform the classical cultures of India, China and the Americas. It was only the Near East which made this leap forward: in technology; in large-scale trade; in irrigation; in the use of writing for economic purposes; in the idea of the territorial city state prevailing over allegiance to traditional clans and lineages; in the cosmological revolution which separated gods from nature. Why this happened only in the Near East towards 3000 BC is one of the great questions of history. For these ideas were transmitted to the later civilizations of the West, developed there and became enshrined as universal experience by the West in the last three centuries: coupled with theories of individual freedom, these are now seen as the driving force of history.

But in the East, and also in the Americas, this split in the psyche of humanity did not take place. There the city and the natural environment remained part of an integrated cosmological structure, which the Chinese for example were able to maintain as a meaningful basis of government right up to the nineteenth century. In the West, the city was an artefact of civilization, a place where laws and institutions sharply distinguished man's identity from that of primeval nature. And now, under the pressure of sheer necessity in a colonial and imperialist age, the rest of the world is trying to catch up with the revolution of five thousand years ago.

TWO

INDIA
EMPIRE OF THE SPIRIT

IN 1856 THE BRITISH ENGINEERS John and William Brunton were engaged in building the East Indian railway from Karachi to Lahore in what is now Pakistan. John Brunton has a curious niche in the history of archaeology. Only two years previously, while constructing army field hospitals in the Dardanelles during the Crimean War, he had employed troops to dig into the mound of Hisarlik: the first excavation on the site of Troy. Now, empire building still further from home on the eve of the Indian 'Mutiny', he had other concerns. The main problems for the railway engineers in the flood plain of the river Indus were how to lay adequate foundations for the track, and where to find ballast. In the south, in Sind, they had hit on an ideal solution: plundering millions of kiln-fired bricks from a great ruined medieval city near Hala. In the north, between Multan and Lahore, the planned line ran close to the mound of another deserted city, known by the name of the village still clinging to its ruins: Harappa. Defended by massive brick fortifications, the citadel stood over the dry bed of an old confluence of the Ravi river; now five miles off, the river was still a great Hindu pilgrimage site in Brunton's day and would remain so right up to partition in 1947. On top of the citadel a Muslim cemetery, a small brick mosque from Moghul times and the shrine of a local Muslim saint co-existed with an old Hindu shrine to the god Siva with lingam and yoni stones (a hint, this, of the possible antiquity of the site, if the Bruntons had paused to think; for the

Muslims had conquered this region in the eighth century AD!) Nevertheless, with that hard-headed gusto typical of Victorian pioneers, the engineers set to work, pulling down the citadel walls to lay the foundations of hundreds of miles of track, over which trains still rumble today.

During the demolition and excavation, the Bruntons' workmen turned up numerous antiquities, including steatite seals engraved with an unknown system of writing, and bearing strange figures of humans, trees and animals, especially bulls. These were shown to a visiting British general who, as chance would have it, would become the director of the Archaeological Survey of India when it was set up in 1861. Alexander Cunningham realized immediately that these finds were quite outside the range of Indian antiquities then known to historians. At that time, Indian history only began with the Mauryan Empire of the late fourth century BC, that is, contemporary with the Hellenistic successors of Alexander the Great. Harappa perplexed Cunningham, and he published some of the seals in the 1870s. But it would be half a century before the mystery of the origin of the seals was solved. In fact, they came from one of the key sites in a great Bronze Age urban civilization whose roots went back thousands of years before historical record; a site whose ancient name had been preserved orally by the people who lived and worshipped on the hill top since the city died in the middle of the second millennium BC.

THE REDISCOVERY OF INDIA'S PREHISTORY

Until the 1920s, the prehistory of India remained a blank. Unlike China, there was no real historiographical tradition in India until the advent of Islam, so there were no written records detailing the chronology of early dynasties or events in a way useful to historians. There were epic poems, like the *Mahabharata* and the *Ramayana*, which harked back to an apparently legendary heroic age, and there were the sacred texts. These sacred books were held by Hindus to have been handed down orally from time immemorial. They had been written down in the Middle Ages in the 'sacred speech', Sanskrit, whose demotic form is the ancestor of most of today's North Indian dialects. Initially, the priestly caste, the Brahmins, who alone memorized and performed the rituals in these texts, were unwilling to let them be seen and copied by non-Brahmins; for them this was sacrilege in itself. (Similarly, Julius Caesar records that the British Druids believed it 'against their principles to commit their doctrines to writing'.) This taboo has been uniquely long-lasting in India. Even in our own time there have been extraordinary cases such as that of an illiterate Brahmin priest who appeared in Benares and dictated a very long religious work in Sanskrit verse, till then unknown and unrecorded, which on internal evidence of style and language was medieval, or even earlier, and which had been passed down orally through a certain line of priests.

Sanskrit began to be known in the West in the seventeenth century, beginning with Roberto de Nobilis and his fascinating attempt to synthesize Hindu and Christian metaphysics in Madurai after 1605. In the eighteenth century, at the same time as the Europeans were becoming heavily embroiled in commercial and military ventures in India, some scholars of the Enlightenment began to be interested in the gods and rituals of India, and to speculate that Hinduism had perhaps been the primeval religion, earlier than any of the monotheisms of the Near East. It was in this intellectual climate in 1786, that a British judge and polymath, Sir William Jones, announced to the Asiatick Society in Calcutta his famous discovery that Sanskrit was related to Latin and Greek through some parent language:

The Sanskrit language, whatever its antiquity, is more perfect than the Greek, more copious than the Latin and more exquisitely refined than either; yet bringing to both of them a stronger affinity than could have been produced by accident; so strong that no philologer could examine all three without believing them to have sprung from some common source, which perhaps no longer exists.

Among the striking parallels Jones made was the identity of the word for father in Greek (*pater*), Latin (*pater*) and in Sanskrit (*pitar*), to which the Germanic *fadar* and modern English *father* were obviously related. Jones himself (whose languages included Welsh and Persian) suggested that the Celtic and Germanic languages were another stem of this 'Indo-European' tree. Remarkable correspondences were subsequently noted in more obscure European tongues: for example, the Sanskrit word for horse, *asva*, is closely matched in Lithuanian by *aszwa*. But if the languages had a common root, did they have a common geographical origin?

Since Jones' day the question of the 'common source' of the Indo-European languages has become both clearer and more complex, and is still hotly disputed by philologists and archaeologists. The majority, however, believe that Sanskrit was not indigenous to India, but originated in a wider Indo-European heartland in south Russia or eastern Europe, from where Sanskrit-speaking peoples migrated into north-west India during the second millennium BC. The track of their migration, indeed, can be recovered. In the fourteenth century BC a dynasty of Indo-European speakers was established in the kingdom of the Mitanni in Upper Mesopotamia. The names of some of their gods are recorded on contemporary clay tablets in forms virtually identical to the Sanskrit: Mitra, Varuna and Indra. Likewise their terminology for chariotry – the classic Indo-European form of warfare – is exactly matched in Sanskrit. At just the same time, around 1400 BC, in north-eastern Iran, on the banks of the Oxus, the prophet Zoroaster had his great revelation, recorded in the *Gathas* in archaic Persian which has many affinities with early Sanskrit. At that time then, these three branches of Indo-European had not long diverged, though no doubt Sanskrit speakers were by then well established in the area of the North-West frontier and the Hindu Kush.

So the Sanskrit-speaking Indo-Europeans came into India from the north-west, establishing themselves around the Kabul river and down into the Punjab, presumably over a long period in the second millennium BC. And in fact the oldest Sanskrit texts enable us to add to this picture. The *Rig Veda* is a series of 1028 hymns and chants which were probably composed over several centuries, between 1500 and 900 BC, though the earliest could just possibly be earlier still. The *Rig Veda* is still sung in Hindu temples today – indeed it is a key part of the coming-of-age ritual of any young Brahmin – and though only committed to writing in the Middle Ages, it has preserved with astonishing accuracy the linguistic forms of the Bronze Age. The earlier verses describe the Sanskrit speakers settled in north-west India, with no hint of migration from outside, so they had clearly been there for some time. They call themselves Aryans, literally 'noble ones' (an Indo-European word which survives in the names of Iran and Eire). Their lands stretch from the Kabul river to the Oxus, along the North-West frontier. Later hymns in the series suggest that by then they had spread into the 'Seven Rivers', today's Punjab. Only in the last of the series is the scene set in the historic heartland of Indian civilization, the valleys of the Ganges and the Jumna. So the *Rig Veda* implies a sequence spanning many centuries, with the expansion of a Sanskrit-speaking aristocracy south-eastwards from the Oxus to the Ganges. But it also shows that the Aryans were not the only people in north-west India in the late Bronze Age, for it often speaks contemptuously of Dasas, Dasyus, or Panias, meaning 'dark-skinned ones' or 'slaves' (recalling the way the early English named their British neighbours *weallas* – Welsh – literally 'slaves'). Evidently the Dasas were an earlier indigenous people; they were 'rich in cattle', they worked gold, they had forts and towns, but were distinguished from the Aryans by speech, looks, and by the colour of their skin. To the evident distaste of the Aryans, they were also *sisna-devi*, 'phallus worshippers.' The *Rig Veda* implies a long period of interaction between the Aryans and the Dasas, at times peaceful, at times warlike, with the destruction of towns and forts. But who were these earlier people?

Such is the tale revealed by the earliest Sanskrit source. And such was the state of knowledge until 1921 when the first scientific excavations began in Sind and Punjab, in the lands of the 'Seven Rivers' of the *Rig Veda*. Until that point it was generally believed that Indian classical culture, and the Hindu religion, were Aryan in origin: a belief no doubt strongly coloured by the pervasive influence of Western theories about the racial and cultural superiority of the Indo-Europeans. Until then it was simply unbelievable that the Aryan civilization had been preceded by a much earlier one, contemporary with those of ancient Iraq and Egypt. But this is precisely what was discovered in 1921–2, pushing back the frontiers of India's history by several thousand years, and making it the oldest known living civilization.

THE LOST CITIES OF THE INDUS

In 1920 excavations started at Harappa under an Indian archaeologist, Daya Ram Sahni, pursuing the clues left by Alexander Cunningham. Despite the damage caused by the Bruntons' depredations, the very first trial diggings produced more seals like those picked up in the 1850s. The upper levels of the site showed occupation during the Mauryan Empire (fourth to third century BC). The deeper levels were obviously prehistoric, but from how far back? The answer came with dramatic swiftness.

The next year, R. D. Banerjee began an excavation at a huge site to the south in Sind: Mohenjo-Daro, the 'Mound of the Dead'. Crowned by a brick stupa from the first century AD, Mohenjo-Daro was apparently a Buddhist ruin, and Buddhist remains were what Banerjee was expecting to find. But almost at once he found evidence of the same prehistoric culture uncovered the previous year at Harappa. The citadel stood on a tract of land called locally 'the Island,' and had been eroded by huge flood channels of the Indus which had gouged a path between it and the eastern suburbs of the ancient city which extended for about a square mile. The finds were among the most spectacular from the ancient world.

About 450 yards long, and probably fortified, the citadel contained an impressive series of ceremonial or governmental buildings including a large columned hall, a huge granary and, most striking of all, a colonnaded tank with a brick-lined bath 40 feet long, 23 feet broad and 8 feet deep which strongly recalled the ritual bathing tanks still seen all over India. Connected to the bath was a large 'college' (as the excavators called it). The temple (if there was one) presumably lay under the Buddhist stupa on the summit of the hill, but this was not removed. In the suburbs were wide streets with grand mansions; there were wells and public latrines for every block; sewers large enough to walk in: this was in some respects a culture more advanced than Egypt or Mesopotamia. And the discovery of seals from Iraq at Mohenjo-Daro dated its heyday to the same period as the flowering of the cities of Sumer – the mid-third millennium BC.

Some aspects of Mohenjo-Daro were puzzling, especially its redbrick uniformity. 'Anyone walking through it for the first time,' wrote the excavator, 'might fancy himself surrounded by the ruins of some present-day working town in Lancashire.' There was barely any sign of exterior decoration, little figural sculpture and the grid plan of the streets was monotonous and regular. 'Stark utilitarianism,' said the final dig report – in short, everything modern India is not! And yet there were also clear signs of a connection with later Indian life. On the seals were sacred trees and animals, including the cow and the hump-backed bull still to be seen nosing inviolate through any crowded Indian bazaar today. Clay models of the mother goddess were like those still made throughout India. A toy bullock cart matched those seen anywhere on the roads of the Punjab today. Most striking of all was a seal depicting a divine figure seated lotus fashion on a deer throne in a yogic posture with bangled arms and a horned head-dress, and surrounded by wild animals. The excavators also believed the figure to be three-faced and ithyphallic, but the seal is so small that these details are not quite certain. All these attributes, though, are very close to those of the great god Shiva in medieval and modern Hinduism, specifically in his role of 'Lord of animals'. Recently there have been attempts to discount the connection of this remarkable image with the later Shiva, but they are unconvincing. No iconography stays still over several millennia; nor do symbols necessarily always retain exactly the same meaning, but that this image is in some sense a 'proto-Shiva' – perhaps in his incarnation as buffalo-god – seems undeniable.

So, like Iraq and Egypt, India had indeed produced a great Bronze Age civilization. And like them it had been literate. Its relation to later history, though, remained problematic. The biggest stumbling block was the writing itself; the key to the identification of the Indus people. Examples of the script had survived engraved on hundreds of seals. But none of the inscriptions was more than a handful of characters, which made decipherment extremely difficult. Indeed, the script remains undeciphered today: one of archaeology's greatest mysteries.

THE INDUS CIVILIZATION

In the last few decades a much fuller picture has emerged of the civilization of Mohenjo-Daro and Harappa. More than a thousand settlements are now known, extending from Afghanistan to Delhi, and from the Himalayan foothills down to Bombay: an area the size of Western Europe, and much larger than either early Iraq or Egypt. Most remarkable, though, is that over this huge area there seems to have been a unity of culture, art, script and technology (and even of weights and measures). The largest city, Mohenjo-Daro, is now thought probably to have reached eighty thousand in population, with five million for the entire state – if state it was. Like Iraq and Egypt its civilization depended on river irrigation. The Indus floods every year, inundating the plain, and on the alluvium they grew wheat, barley, rice and cotton, which seems to have been cultivated in Sind for the first time in history (hence its name in Greek – *sindon*). The Indus civilization also depended on long-distance trade, shipping cotton, hardwoods, ivory and precious stones to

Sumerian cities like Ur, where there was a colony of Indus merchants in the third millennium BC. Indus seals found in Sumer often carry the marks of the bales of merchandise to which they were affixed. This trade with the Persian Gulf region is one of the oldest international connections in Indian culture. A Greek merchant's manual from around 60 AD describes sandalwood, ebony, cotton, spices and pearls coming to the Gulf from Gujerat. This same produce was the mainstay of the trade between Basra and India in the Ottoman and British periods, and the Indian trade with Iraq remains unbroken today.

THE DEEPER ROOTS: NEW EXCAVATIONS IN BALUCHISTAN

Our understanding of the origins of the Indus cities has been transformed in the last thirty years by excavations at Mehrgarh near Quetta in north-west Pakistan. Here, the story of settled continuous occupation in the Indus region has been taken back to the seventh millennium BC, four thousand years before the flowering of the Harappan age; back into the same period when agricultural communities were forming across the Near East from Palestine to Iran. As late as the 1970s there was no evidence of agriculture in India much before 3000 BC, underlining what a revolution these finds have brought. These discoveries reveal the great antiquity of not only the farming economy in the Indus valley, but also of craft specialization (including steatite cutting), and of long-distance trade (in turquoise and lapis). In the fifth millennium BC builders at Mehrgarh used the long plano-convex brick we find later in the Indus cities; and cotton was already cultivated. In the fourth millennium BC the little town was part of a wide common cultural zone extending into Iran. In about 2500 BC it was abandoned, superseded by a large town five miles away at Naushahro which had massive brick fortifications and impressive buildings including a possible temple. By then we are into the Harappan age proper.

These new discoveries make it absolutely certain that the

Indus civilization was an Indian phenomenon, growing out of the native prehistoric cultures of its region, and not, as was thought in some quarters, stimulated by diffusion of cultural ideas from Iraq. But who were the people of the Indus civilization, if they were not Aryan Indo-Europeans? Were they the Dasas of the *Rig Veda*? A new picture has begun to emerge, only since the 1980s. The crucial discovery has been the proving beyond any doubt, that the ancient pre-Aryan language of Iran, Elamite, is cognate with the ancient Dravidian languages still spoken in Southern India, best known of which is Tamil. These languages descend from a prehistoric speech spoken in Iran and north-western India, and doubtless in the early villages like Mehrgarh: indeed a pocket of a related language, Brahui, is still spoken today in a small area of West Pakistan on the Iranian border. The original proto-language split up around 5000 BC, at a guess, after the invention of agriculture, to judge by its common terminology in Elamite and Dravidian. The Elamite branch was spoken in the early urban societies in Iran contemporary with Sumer around 3000 BC, and ceased to be spoken in the tenth century AD. Dravidian is still spoken now by over 200 million South Indians.

This has tremendous implications for the whole history of early India. For it suggests that Dravidian languages are not native to the south, but moved from Baluchistan through Gujerat and into Southern India only after about 5000 BC. There the early Dravidians found ancient tribes who still live in the forests stretching down into Andra and across into Orissa, and who still preserve older forms of religion and social organization. Once rooted in the south, the Dravidians developed towns and rediscovered writing only in the late first millennium BC.

The proving of these linguistic links transforms our understanding of the Indus civilization, for it makes it virtually certain that an early form of Dravidian, related to modern Tamil, was spoken in the Indus valley at the time of Mohenjo-Daro and Harappa. Hence, most probably, the undeciphered inscriptions on the seals are Dravidian, as scholars have long suspected. Other fascinating pieces of evidence back this up, from the survival of Dravidian kinship terminology in today's Gujerat to the continued presence of Dravidian-derived custom in the Indus region. One tiny detail will serve as an example: on Hindu pilgrim stalls in Madurai, South India, the symbol of the town's goddess Minakshi is a fish with stars. Her name comes from the most ancient stratum of Tamil: '*min*' means both 'fish' and 'star', ancient symbols of divinity. This combination is depicted on Harappan pottery and seals; but it is also still found on Muslim pilgrim stalls in Sind where the fish is carved with the Muslim creed – an amazing testimony to the tenacity of religious symbols over time!

Eighty years after the discovery of Harappa, the strands are beginning to come together. The Indus civilization was almost certainly Dravidian, its culture closely related to the Elamite world of Iran, and distantly related to today's culture in South India. It declined around 1700 BC, through a combination of factors which may have included a marked decrease in rainfall and the collapse of long-distance trade. The big cities were abandoned, though smaller settlements continued later. At the same time the Indo-European Aryans who had conquered Iran were expanding into the mountainous zone between the Oxus and the Indus, and over a long period of time they became the dominant culture and speech in the Sind and Punjab, completely assimilating the native Dravidian speakers (though loan-words in the Sanskrit of the *Rig Veda* testify to their presence). Between 1500 and 1000 BC the Aryans spread into the Ganges and Jumna valleys, burning the forests, building settlements and cultivating the land. In the meantime Dravidian language and culture had spread into South India where we can trace continuity back to 3000 BC. It was out of the interaction of these two cultures that the civilizations of classical India would emerge. This is a tentative reconstruction as yet, but its basic outline is surely right.

THE HEROIC AGE

For a long period after the decline of the Indus civilization, perhaps for as much as a thousand years, there was no true urban life in India. North Indian society was rural, ruled by various Aryan chieftains who settled along the river valleys surrounded by vast tracts of forest inhabited by the aboriginal population, the Adivasis, whose tribal descendants still live there today. It may have been during this period that the caste system began to take shape, a form of social segregation based on an elaborately graded hierarchy – from Brahmins (priests) at the top, to the 'untouchables' at the bottom, who for example dispose of the dead. The original meaning of caste (*varna*) is colour, and perhaps the system began as a way of keeping the light-skinned Aryans apart from the darker-skinned native population. The epic poem *Mahabharata*, though written down much later, preserves genuine traditions of this time. It tells of warring Aryan clans in the Ganges valley, sacking each other's citadels and seizing women, cattle and treasure, much like the heroic age portrayed by Homer's *Iliad*. In some cases modern archaeology has confirmed the basic tale. The Kaurava capital in the *Mahabharata*, for example, was Hastinapur on the Ganges, which excavation in the 1950s showed to have been destroyed by flooding in about 800 BC. This event is actually described in one of the Sanskrit religious texts as taking place in the time of the seventh king to rule there since the great war of the *Mahabharata*, which dates that war quite plausibly to about 900 BC. Some of the traditions of that time have been very long-lasting: the scene of the *Mahabharata*'s climactic battle, Kurukshetra, is still an important pilgrimage place today.

The *Mahabharata* also suggests that the sacred geography of India was well established during the first millennium BC, in a pattern which has remained ever since; indeed the concept of India as one motherland united by pilgrimage may come from this time. The poem contains a list of 270 holy places which form a circuit of the entire country. The last, and most famous, was

Prayag, now Allahabad at the junction of the Ganges and Jumna.

Allahabad is still the site of a great religious festival each year, and every twelfth year, at the Kumbh Mela, it sees the largest gathering of humanity anywhere on earth. In February 1989, fifteen million were present on the most auspicious night, many more over the whole month of the festival. Just such a gathering with half a million pilgrims was witnessed here in 644 AD by the Chinese Buddhist pilgrim Hsuan Tsang, who was told it had gone on since ancient times. Fascinating new research has shown why Prayag had pre-eminent sanctity as the 'king of holy places'. Prayag was viewed as the navel of the earth, the mythical creation point of the universe, just like Eridu, Delphi, or Cuzco: the site of the primordial mound which rose out of the waters (a phenomenon still to be seen at Allahabad at Mela time as the flood water of the Ganges subsides). Here was an archaic pillar cult at the point where heaven and earth were first separated, and a sacred 'undying' tree like that at Eridu (or the Biblical Garden of Eden) which was seen by Hsuan Tsang in 644; still alive in the seventeenth century, it is now a stump only. In the period of the epics, the first millennium BC, the chief cult shrines at Prayag stood on an island whose outline can still be seen although the Ganges has changed its course over the centuries. On the north end of the island was a shrine to the primordial serpent who protected the eternal tree. It is still there today, the only one of its kind in India.

THE GANGES CIVILIZATION

Towards 600 BC a number of settled kingdoms had come into existence in the Ganges valley, and large cities began once more to be built in India. Some of them had great ditch and rampart systems. Kausambi, for example, near Allahabad, had a five-mile circuit with eleven gates and large public buildings. Its walls were constructed in burned bricks of standard size, and their huge sloping revetments strikingly recall those at Harappa, though it is hard to see how such a tradition could have been passed down directly. These cities became important centres of long–distance

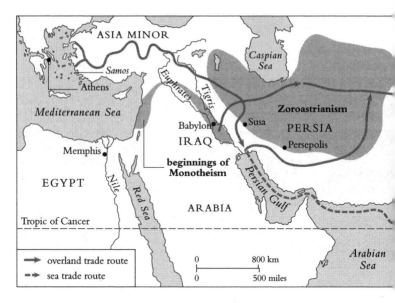

Above: The Axis Age, c.500 BC. In a few decades on either side of 500 BC
the Buddha and Mahavira were alive in India, Confucius (and Lao Tzu?) in
China, the greatest of the Hebrew prophets in Palestine and Babylonia,
along with early Greek scientists and philosophers and the founders of
Athenian democracy: the spiritual legacy of the Bronze Age was being
revalued.

Right: Medieval India, showing the Moghul Empire under Akbar.
The South continued to go its own way, as it had under the Cholas
(c.900–1300) and before: the most ancient cultural and linguistic divide in
Indian history.

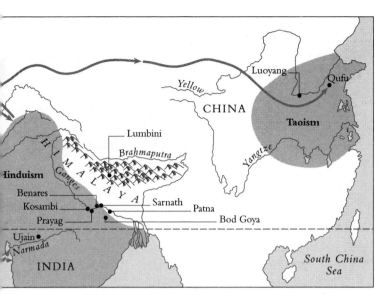

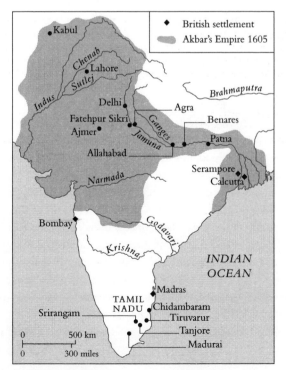

trade, and in them in the sixth century BC a great ferment of spiritual and intellectual ideas took place. The chief focus of this brilliant and exciting time was a city which has remained India's greatest centre of learning and culture to this day: Benares or Kashi, 'City of Light'.

The early history of Benares is very sketchily known. In the archaeological record it begins with the remains of a burned brick wall and ditch from the eighth century BC on the high plateau where the British built their railway bridge in 1887. Only in the Middle Ages did it spread south to today's magnificent three-mile frontage along the Ganges. By the third century BC, it was said to be 'the chief city in all India' and by then had gained its reputation as the city of Shiva. How this happened is not certain: despite the evidence from the Indus valley, the origin of Shiva is still a mystery and should probably be sought in the indigenous prehistoric cultures of North India. The recent find of a goddess shrine south of Allahabad, dated to 11000 BC and constructed exactly as is still done in tribal culture, is a hint at the immense antiquity of traditional Indian religion: Mesolithic cave paintings of a dancing shaman with horned head-dress, bangles and trident, closely resembling Shiva, suggest that god's long prehistory.

In the sixth century BC, the Ganges cities produced an astonishing intellectual and religious flowering. Writing was re-introduced, having vanished with the Indus cities; the new script, Brahmi, was adapted from that of the Persian empire and is the ancestor of all subsequent Indian scripts. A prodigious amount of material comes from this time: astronomy, geometry, grammar, phonetics, etymology, but especially religion and philosophy. This was a time of great speculation about the creation of the world, culminating in the *Upanishads*, one of India's great legacies to the world. Out of the ancient pre-Aryan animism and Aryan sacrificial religion, Indian civilization had moved to the subtlest reaches of thought, and from that time till today there is an unbroken continuity of that kind of spiritual exploration which is so characteristic of Indian civilization.

Many different sects arose in what was clearly an atmosphere of deep spiritual unrest, especially among the rising class of merchants in the cities who were least attracted by Aryan religion. All rejected the sacrificial polytheism of the Aryans; most opposed caste and ritual too. Such thinkers seem to represent a recognition of the rule of natural law in the universe, rather like their contemporaries, the natural philosophers of Ionian Greece. Among their gurus were atheists, rationalists, sceptics, and out-right materialists like Ajita Kesakambalin who rejected any notion of the afterlife. Kassapa Kaccayana's atomic theories, and his assertion that all change is illusory, remind us particularly strongly of the pre-Socratic Greeks like Heraclitus of Ephesus. All these strands can be found in medieval and modern Hinduism. But the two greatest religious movements of the Ganges civilization were the Jains and the Buddhists.

BUDDHISM AND JAINISM

Four miles away from the gaudy tumult of Benares, in about 500 BC, a young Indian prince preached a sermon which would change the world. His name was Gautama, but we know him as his followers did, as the Buddha, the 'Enlightened One'. 'I have reached the conviction,' he said, 'that human suffering must be comprehended.' His answer to the perennial question of life was simple and typically Indian. 'It is attachment to the senses and to material desires,' he said, 'which is the root of all human unhappiness. Get rid of those desires and you will find the path to salvation.' This bleak, essentially atheistic message would spread across Asia to China, Korea and Japan, where it remains a fundamental force to this day.

The Buddha (563–483 BC) was not the only reformer. Mahavira, the last guru of the Jains, who died around 477 BC, was his contemporary. Jainism, like Buddhism, is atheistic in nature, the existence of God being irrelevant to belief. For Jains, everything in the universe has a soul. Hence they practise an austere form of non-violence and vegetarianism. Unlike Buddhism, Jainism has an unbroken tradition in India especially among the merchant communities of Western India. Some have speculated, indeed, that it ultimately derives, however indirectly, from the mercantile communities of the Indus. It has continued with vitality until today: Mahavira's teachings were recycled in the ethics of Gandhi, brought up in a Banias trader caste in the Jain culture of Gujerat.

Both Buddhism and Jainism were characterized by a rejection of Brahmin civilization with its caste divisions and its sacrificial cult (and its Indo-European hierarchy of male gods). They represent a transition from the magical thought of the Vedas to a new kind of rationality, exemplified in the Buddha's 'four noble truths' and his eightfold path to salvation which rested on individual morality and action. Both too were tinged with pessimism, notably in the Buddha's view of life as an intolerable chain of suffering from which mankind can only break free by extinguishing earthly desire. It was a vision of the human condition as distinctive of India as tragedy and philosophy were of the Greeks; indeed when we consider the Buddha sitting lotus fashion in his deer park under the sacred pipal tree, 'lord of the animals', just like the enigmatic 'proto-Shiva' on the Indus seal, we may wonder how far such a figure, renouncing the material world, goes back into the Indian past.

It may be no coincidence that the Buddha arose at this moment. The historian Karl Jaspers called the period of the Buddha's lifetime, from the sixth to the fifth century BC, the Axis Age, because so many of the great thinkers in world history were alive at the same time: the Buddha and Mahavira in India; Pythagoras, Heraclitus and the early Greek philosophers; the greatest of the Old Testament prophets, in particular 'Deutero-Isaiah'; Confucius, Lao Tzu and the Taoists in China. It is extraordinary to think that some of those people could actually have met each other! This coincidence of lives suggests that the ancient world which had emerged from the first civilizations of Iraq and Egypt, China and India, was undergoing a crisis of spirit. Fundamental questions were being asked about the nature of God, about the purpose of life on earth and about the basis of

The Garden of Eden? In the marshes between the Tigris and Euphrates in South Iraq was a world of tiny islands with reed houses unchanged in millennia until recently. This is where ancient Babylonian and biblical myth placed the Creation.

Top: The 'Royal Standard' of Ur – the wealth of civilization is brought to the king. Made from inlaid lapis lazuli on wood, it dates from c.2700 BC.
Above: The diversity of the Iraqi tradition – Yezidis grew out of the mingling of Christian, Jewish and Islamic ideas in the Middle Ages. Manichaean dualism is part of their belief; for them, Satan is first to be propitiated.
Opposite: The spiral minaret at Samarra – an early Islamic echo of the Tower of Babel? Built in the eighth century AD, it is 164 feet high.

Top: Roots of Indian tradition – the 'sacred' bath at Mohenjo-Daro, Pakistan.
Above: The Kumbh Mela festival at the confluence of the Ganges and the
Jumna rivers. The festival dates from the twelfth century AD but the site is
of immemorial sanctity.
Opposite top: The river front on the Ganges at Benares. 'There are many
holy places on this wide earth, but which one of them equals one speck of
Kashni's dust?'
Opposite bottom: Portuguese Jesuits debating with Muslim holy men
before Akbar. 'His court became the home of the enquirers of the seven
climes and the meeting place of every religion and sect' (Abul Fazl).

Above: Moghul civilization –
the Taj Mahal at Agra, a
seventeenth-century royal
tomb situated in a paradise
garden on the Jumna river.
Right: The South Indian
tradition – a gateway to
the great temple of Shiva
Nataraja at Chidambaram,
Tamil Nadu.
Opposite, top left: Fawang
temple on the sacred
mountain, Songshan, one
of the earliest Buddhist
shrines in China (71 AD).
Opposite, top right: Visionary
art from Dunhuang (eighth
century AD), one of a
thousand caves decorated
between the third and
thirteeth centuries AD.
Opposite bottom: The
Longmen caves near the
ancient capital of Luoyang,
a vast collection of Buddhist
monuments built between
500 and 900 AD.

Top: A Silk Route landscape. The Lake of the Crescent Moon lies amongst immense sand dunes outside Dunhuang.
Above: European partners cutting up the Chinese cake – a French cartoon from 1898.

the authority of the kings and states. And at the heart of it all were the questions which still plague governments today, even in sophisticated, technocratic societies like the United States and Western Europe – all the more now perhaps, when the sanction of religion has lost its power to teach or frighten. How do you persuade your citizens to act as moral beings? How do you persuade them to be good? The different ways in which those early civilizations attempted to come to terms with these questions still shape their descendants, and us, today. The Near East took the path of monotheism which would become central to the ideology of the West, as well as of Islam. China held to the Confucian conception of the individual, the family and the state in a perfectable moral order on earth. In India the great tradition asserted that attachment to this earthly material life is illusion and that true enlightenment can only come by forsaking it: the very opposite of Western thinking. And so the social and economic character of these great cultures is still touched by that revolutionary epoch even today.

THE MAURYAN EMPIRE

In the fourth century BC came the first attempt to impose a political unity on India: the Mauryan Empire. And from this time comes the first Western account of India, written by a Greek ambassador, Megasthenes. Arriving at the Mauryan capital at Patna on the Ganges, the Greeks were stunned to find the largest city of the ancient world. A 22-mile rectangle with 570 towers, 64 gates and a population of 400,000: bigger than Rome at its height. They were surprised too, to find that – unlike Greece – India was not a slave-based society, though the regimented government was a far cry from the genial anarchy of today's Patna. Chandragupta Maurya, whose court Megasthenes visited, is said to have been a Jain, and to have ended his life by resigning and fasting to death, as great holy men did in the Jain tradition. His grandson Ashoka expanded the empire further to include much of India. But it is not for conquests that Ashoka's thirty-five-year reign is remembered as one of the most extraordinary in world history. Ashoka's story can be pieced together in his own words from inscriptions on stone columns like that at Kausambi which is still today an object of veneration for Buddhist pilgrims from Korea, Japan and Tibet. It was after a victorious war in Orissa, he says, in which he killed a hundred thousand people, that Ashoka became convinced that war was wrong. Then he turned to the idea which would echo across the ages right down to Mahatma Gandhi: *ahimsa*, non-violence. 'From now on,' he said, 'I will try to conquer by right conduct alone.'

All across India, from the Khyber to the southern Deccan, Ashoka had his edicts inscribed, often using the ancient Hindu cosmic pillars which already existed at sites of immemorial sanctity, such as Prayag and Sarnath, where the Buddha had preached his first sermon. These archaic symbols were transformed, literally, into pillars of morality, explaining what the doctrine of *dharma*, 'right conduct', actually meant. Remarkably, it was not based on the sanction of religious authority. It was a secular ideal of the dignity of human beings, and of the humanistic possibilities of civic morality, based on the Buddhist eightfold path of 'right thinking' and the Jain belief in non-violence. 'I have honoured men of all creeds,' said Ashoka. 'But I consider this to be the essential thing, what I call "the approach through one's own free will."' On the pillar edicts appear all those words which modern politicians find so difficult to pronounce today: compassion, tolerance, gentleness, truthfulness. The clauses on non-violence abjure meat-eating and preserve a whole range of species from the parrot to the white ant, from the Ganges porpoise to the rhinoceros. 'Forests,' Ashoka said with prophetic force, 'must not be burned uselessly.' In his ecological and conservation measures, Ashoka sounds astonishingly modern to us today, no doubt misleadingly so. We are impressed, too, by his wide-ranging social and welfare legislation. But there is also an ominously contemporary ring, in that bane of our own time, massive state intervention, with an army of spies and thought police to check up on what people were doing. It sounds intolerable to us today – and no doubt it was to some people of the time too! But Ashoka is an extraordinary product of that extraordinary age, the Axis Age, in his turning away from the authority of religion and magic to that of reason and morality as a basis for politics. And however imperfectly he tried to execute it, his idea of *dharma*, right conduct, was one of the great ideas of human history to set beside Greek democracy, the American Bill of Rights, the Communist Manifesto. Indeed, as the troubled twentieth century draws to its close, one might be forgiven for thinking that this was an idea whose time is almost come! After Indian Independence in 1948, Ashoka's lion from his pillar at Sarnath was taken as the emblem of India. Nothing could be more appropriate.

UNITY IN DIVERSITY

Ashoka's political order did not survive, but his empire had opened up communications in India by land and sea. From the first century AD, drawn by India's wealth, Mediterranean merchants flocked there on the monsoon winds. From ports like Cochin, in Kerala, Arab traders bore some of India's greatest scientific discoveries to the West, including her most brilliant invention, the mathematical system of nine digits and zero which we all use today. But the real motive for the trade was spice.

In the trading post of Cochin, for centuries foreign merchants bought the famed spices of the Malabar coast, especially pepper and ginger, which are both originally south Indian words. Such contacts helped breed an outward-looking and tolerant society, as Kerala still is. Many foreign merchants came here and settled, becoming Indian, even if they retained their own religion. Evidence of their presence is found every-where up the little rivers and creeks in the Cochin backwaters. Tradition says the Jews came to Kerala from Iraq in the sixth century BC. Tamil and Sanskrit loan words in the Hebrew Bible suggest tradition could be right: they were certainly here by Roman times. At Parur is one of the oldest and loveliest synagogues in the world. It is maintained by only one family now, carefully performing the rites as best they can. Recently local girls have converted to marry into the family, so they still hope their traditions will be passed on. Near Parur, at Chendamangalam, the synagogue is now closed, but next door is a thriving church of the Syrian Christians, who claim they were founded by the Apostle Thomas himself. It was to this coast that King Alfred of Wessex was said to have sent alms in the ninth century all the way from Viking Age England! Islam meanwhile came here peacefully by sea in the seventh century with Arab traders, not as elsewhere by war and conquest; today in a beautiful little wooden pillared mosque with a tiny bathing tank, the Muslim children of the village learn the classical Arabic of the Koran by rote. So here today in Chendamangalam, Hindu, Christian, Muslim and Jew live side by side. 'All these people of different faiths,' says Krishna in the *Gita*, 'whatever form of worship they choose to fulfil their desires, ultimately their worship comes back to the same source.'

THE COMING OF ISLAM

Hinduism, Buddhism and Jainism are all indigenous to India, and all, as we have seen, drew on deep roots. From India they (especially Buddhism) spread to Asia and the world. By the ninth century AD, though, Buddhism was practically wiped out within India, largely because its ideas were absorbed back into mainstream Hindu thought by reformers like the brilliant young philosopher from Kerala, Adi Shankara. Henceforth the Buddha would be more commonly seen on the pilgrim stalls of Indian cities as one of the incarnations of the god Vishnu. Jainism on the other hand was able to survive within the Hindu tradition. But the coming of Islam, which would become the second religion of India in terms of numbers and importance, was a revolutionary event which broke the ancient bonds between India and its indigenous religious systems.

Initially Islam was brought to India towards the close of the seventh century, by Muslim traders travelling old routes long used by Arab seafarers, to the Indus and to Kerala, where the oldest Muslim community in India is believed to be and where the Muslim faith easily found a hold. But in northern India however, the impact of Islam was very different. 'India is full of riches,' wrote the Muslim historian Al Biruni, 'entirely beautiful and delightful, and as its people are mainly infidels and idolaters, it is right by order of God, for us to conquer them.' Within a few decades of the prophet's death, Islam had swept westwards to Spain and eastwards to the Indus valley. Sind was taken in 711 AD. Then a long and bitter struggle ensued between the newest and the oldest faith. Eventually Muslim attacks shattered the old Hindu kingdoms of the north. Benares itself fell in 1194, and many of the city's most famous Hindu temples would be sacked and demolished time and again over the next few centuries: a tale repeated in all the pilgrim cities of the north as periods of tolerance alternated with bouts of persecution by the Muslim rulers of the medieval sultanates of Delhi and the Deccan. These tragedies initiated a long and tortuous relationship between Hindu and Muslim which both enriched India and which even in our own time has threatened to tear it apart. The early arrival of Sufism in Sind, for example, was the beginning of one of the richest strands of Indian Islam which has had a profound influence on the whole of Indian religious life, even today. In time, Indian Islam was 'Hinduised': in India Mohammed's biography could become a variation on the Hindu Krishna story, and Imam Hussayn, the martyr of Kerbala, could be portrayed as an avatar of the god Vishnu among the thriving Shiite communities which grew up in cities like Lucknow.

In Benares, the sacred city of the Hindus, the Muslims became the mainstay of the city's economy; the thousands of silk weavers, with their tiny shops and hand looms, are all Muslim. It was here in the fifteenth century that the poor weaver Kabir preached the brotherhood of Hindu and Muslim. Kabir was born into a Muslim community in Benares – his name is Muslim – but the major influence on his life was from the Hindu followers of Vishnu and their *bhakti* devotional movement which saw God (whom Kabir called Ram, not Allah) as love: 'Reading book after book, the whole world died. And none ever became learned. He who can decipher just a syllable of "love" is the true pandit.'

Like many great religious thinkers Kabir rejected the externals of religious practice, in his case both Hindu and Muslim. He rejected Muslim prayer ritual and Hindu image worship; the Muslim Haj to Mecca, and the Hindu pilgrimage to Benares; Muslim circumcision and the Brahmin sacred thread (on the interesting grounds that they exclude women). All were a hindrance to the expression of true religion which he saw as a matter of personal experience. Kabir attracted a large following among Hindus and Muslims. But as so often in history, the legacy of such great figures becomes dogged by sectarianism. The modern Kabiri sect regard themselves as Hindu, though they still maintain their monotheism and a strong ethical code, and they oppose caste and image worship. Kabir's was the most thorough-going, grassroots attempt in the Middle Ages to bridge the divide between the religions and, in a typically Indian way, was deeply rooted in the past.

So Islam became an integral part of the diversity of India, transforming India and Hinduism and transformed in its turn. India's 100 million Muslim people make it the second largest Muslim country in the world, even after the partition of Bangladesh and Pakistan. These tremendous events are still working themselves out. The secular constitution of 1950, based on European models, attempted to set the seal on the ancient wounds and enmities of the past, but religion is still the great power in India for good and ill and she has not escaped sectarian strife since Independence. Indeed, now that the dust has settled, the conflicting claims of different gods (and social classes) have become all the more clamorous. In the 1990s a rising tide of Hindu fundamentalism saw riots and the wrecking of the weavers' shops in the old Muslim quarter of Benares. Thousands of looms were smashed, and lives were ruined as India's ideal of unity in diversity went through a new ordeal of fire – an ordeal from which it now appears to have emerged.

THE MOGHUL EMPIRE

In the sixteenth century, the mixed Muslim and Hindu culture which arose in the north gave birth to yet another brilliant flowering of Indian civilization – the Muslim dynasty of the Moghuls. Originally from the high plateau between Persia and Afghanistan, the Moghuls created a great land empire with a centralized administration which laid the basis of the later British and modern Indian states.

The Moghul empire also created an art and architecture which still defines our popular image of India today in its flamboyant mixture of Hindu, Persian and Muslim, symbolized by the Taj Mahal and the city of Fatehpur Sikri, founded in 1569 near Agra by Akbar the Great. Emperor and Generalissimo, Akbar was a noble patron of the arts and literature, and commissioned a translation of the *Mahabharata* into Persian, along with many wonderful painted manuscripts. Like other rulers of India before and after, he came to understand that the only way to rule India, indeed any civilization, is with tolerance and pluralism and increasingly he was drawn to the deepest currents in Indian thought.

The most fascinating aspect of Akbar's career was his attempt to find a synthesis of all the religions in his empire. It could only ever have happened, perhaps, in the heady religious climate of India. And it is all the more remarkable because Akbar was brought up a devout Muslim, and was illiterate; his tutors unanimously condemned him as a bad pupil! But impressed by the terrible evils which are unleased by religious intolerance (and perhaps not unmindful of political considerations) Akbar summoned holy men from the Hindus and the Jains, the Christians and the Jews, the Zoroastrians, even Mandaeans from Persia along with Sunni and Shia Muslims. Out of their discussions he attempted to formulate a simple belief in God, a 'doctrine of right conduct' which strangely echoes Ashoka, even though Akbar knew nothing of him nor, it seems, of Buddhism. Akbar was even prepared to acknowledge the rightness of the case for vegetarianism, although as a good meat-eating Moghul that was one aspect that he was unable to fulfil in his personal life! This belief in God, so Akbar hoped, could be a simple, basic moral guide for the élite in his empire of so many religions. Nothing quite like it had ever happened before in history.

All the strands of the story come together in an extraordinary incident which has only recently come to light. In January 1575 Akbar travelled with his closest Hindu adviser to Prayag, 'king of pilgrimage places', for the great bathing festival. He had already launched his campaign for a new 'belief in God' (*Din-i Ilaha*), and now he renamed Prayag *Ilah-abas*, a mixture of Arabic and Hindu meaning 'the place of God'. So was the primal creation place in Hindu mythology deliberately chosen as a centre of the new religion? Was the new *dharma*, like the old of Ashoka, to be proclaimed and guaranteed from the cosmic centre with its *axis mundi* and its Tree of Life? Remarkably, Akbar would go on to construct a vast fortress residence around the 'undying tree' and the 'Ashokan' pillar of laws at Allahabad (as it would later become known). His apartments were built above the holy tree, looking out over the spot where, as his biographer relates, 'most strangely, when Jupiter enters the constellation of Aquarius, a small mound appears out of the Ganges, remaining for one month; and here the people offer worship.'

One of his friends at court said that Akbar had the one quality which makes a ruler truly great, namely 'the capacity to meet people of whatever rank or whatever religion with the same eye of favour.' His tolerance would be remarkable even today, but in the sixteenth century was astonishing. At that time Western Europe, for example, was torn apart by religious wars, with unspeakable cruelties being done to people in the name of God. Akbar's moving and sincere attempt to express the divine in a combination of Islam, Christianity and Upanishadic Hinduism was perhaps doomed to failure, but his insight into the Indian predicament was not lost on Nehru, nor on Mahatma Gandhi, who insisted that 'all religions are true.' In Fatehpur Sikri at the Gate of Victory, this great son of a great Muslim dynasty left us this enigmatic epitaph. 'Jesus, peace be on him, said this, "The world is a bridge, cross it but build no house upon it, the world endures for but an hour, spend it in devotion, the rest is unseen."'

Akbar's city of dreams was deserted because of lack of water. Today Fatehpur Sikri lies high and dry on its ridge near Agra looking over a parched red plain. His empire had created a unified state giving the same rights to Muslim and Hindu. An empire of the sword had succumbed to the empire of the spirit. 'In the past,' said Akbar, 'to our shame, we forced many Hindus to adopt the faith of our ancestors. Now it has become clear to me, that in our troubled world so full of contradictions, it cannot be wisdom to assert the unique truth of one faith over another. The wise person makes justice his guide and learns from all. Perhaps in this way the door may be opened again, whose key has been lost.'

DARA SHUKOH: THE DREAM IS LOST

In the heartland of India, fifty years after Akbar's death, two Moghul royal brothers, his great-grandsons, fought a battle over his legacy whose effects are still with us today. The issue was the course Indian Islam should take. The elder, Dara Shukoh, the disciple of radical Sufis, was impressed not only by the most problematic figure in Islam – Hallaj, but by the Hindu *Bhagavad Gita*. The younger brother, Aurangzeb, was educated by legalists and orthodox Sufis, the converting order who had made much headway converting Hindus in Kashmir and Bengal.

Dara went further than Akbar. A scholar of the religious classics of Islam and Hinduism, he took his stand on the Koran's revelation that God had sent messengers to all peoples and given them their scriptures (as indeed the god Krishna says in the *Gita*). Dara then insisted that it was the moral duty of Muslims to learn from other religions, indeed that the 'concealed scriptures' of Surah 56 of the Koran were none other than the *Upanishads*: the original core of monotheism. Dara translated the *Gita* and some of the *Upanishads* into Persian. (Put into Latin in Paris in 1802, his version was part of the influx into the West of Hindu mysticism, which inspired Blake and Schopenhauer among others – but that is another story!) Dara maintained that his translation was intended to clarify the Koranic revelation, not to devalue it. He also wrote a *Lives of Muslim Saints* and a treatise on comparative religion, *The Meeting of the Two Oceans*, in which he tried to prove the equivalence of technical vocabulary of Sufi and Hindu mysticism.

Needless to say, such syncretistic leanings did not go down well with the ruling Muslim orthodoxy, for whom the Koranic message was complete and could neither be added to nor taken away from. Dara's younger brother Aurangzeb felt he had 'become a kaffir' and induced the lawyers to pronounce him apostate for claiming, among other things, that Hinduism and Islam were 'twin brothers'. Defeated in a civil war, Dara was murdered in 1659. Gifted as he was as a ruler, Aurangzeb's long reign (he died in 1707) left a bitter memory among Hindus, for he destroyed scores of their temples including the greatest shrines to Shiva and Vishnu in Benares; a legacy now being exploited by Hindu fundamentalists.

In fact, the experiments of Akbar and Dara Shukoh were not a total failure: some Indian Sufi orders, for example, changed their attitude to Hinduism, allowing a fruitful crossover, as there had been among the *bhakti* devotional poets of the Middle Ages. But if these remarkable Moghuls had succeeded, then perhaps Hinduism might have evolved on a path more in line with its monotheistic potential (as it did under the impact of Christianity in the nineteenth century). Indeed Indian Islam might even have become absorbed into it, rather as Buddhism and Jainism had been. But this did not happen, and the great struggle to reach accommodation and understanding still continues.

THE SOUTH

In the far south of India, a verdant and fecund land of temples, the ancient Dravidian culture of the Tamils escaped the full Muslim impact. And here the Hindu vision of unity survived. Far into the tropics, nearly 2000 miles south of the snowy peaks of Kashmir, Tamil Nadu was a rich rice-growing region whose wealth was based on the massive irrigation works of the Cauvery river delta. Marco Polo called it 'the most splendid province in the world,' and its distinctive culture had roots going back far into prehistory. Separated from the north by race and language, the Tamils exemplify India's search for unity in diversity.

The Tamil shore, the Coromandel coast, was frequented by Greek and Roman traders. 'Here,' said a Tamil poet, 'beautiful great ships of the Greeks bearing gold came splashing on the white foam to return laden with spices.' And in their turn the Tamils would later take Hindu culture as far as Java and Cambodia, spreading the empire of the spirit to become the dominant culture of south-east Asia: islands like Bali are still Hindu today.

Here in the ninth century a powerful state arose under the Chola dynasty who left a brilliant legacy in poetry, painting and sculpture. It was King Aditya (871–907) who laid the foundation, 'building a row of great stone temples to Shiva down the banks of the Cauvery river all the way from the elephant-haunted Sahya mountains down to the ocean which has the moon playing on the folds of its restless waves.' These temples are among the finest of all Indian architecture. Some of the shrines were already famous in the sixth century AD, and would be expanded and embellished to become the greatest temple cities in India, if not in the world. They are still renowned pilgrimage centres today, places such as Tiruvarur, Srirangam, and Chidambaram, the home of the Cholan royal cult to Shiva as the dancing god. Chidambaram represents the accretion of many layers of India's cultic past: Dravidian, Aryan and aboriginal. Sacred tree, holy tank, tiger shrine, primordial lingam, primeval goddess, aboriginal Tamil dancing god: all found their place here. Its tiny core is a ninth-century wooden hall covered with gilded tiles surrounded by the vast towers and halls of the Chola age. In its treasury are many bronzes from that time, for this was the heyday of the ancient Indian craft of bronze casting which stretches back to the Indus cities. One group of master craftsmen, possibly a single family, worked for a small temple in the Cauvery delta at Tiruvengadu where no less than thirty bronzes cast in the early eleventh century have survived the vagaries of time and war. They deal with themes of great antiquity: Shiva as the dancing god, the great yogi, or the androgyne, and the great goddess in both her terrible and benign aspects: themes still capable of potent reinvention even today in the cinema or on television. Among their masterpieces is an image of Shiva in his archaic role as lord of the animals. But here the wild god of prehistory is transformed by the Tamil sensibility into a sinuous and sensuous cowherd with a turban of snakes. This was cast in one piece by the lost wax process in 1011. There had been nothing like it since the ancient Greeks.

The cultural centre of the southern Tamils from ancient Greek times was Madurai, 'the splendid temple with its tall towers,' as a poet sang. Since the days of Megasthenes the Greeks had known Madurai as a thriving city, and a great commercial entrepôt; a city of shrines 'whose citizens rise not to the lark but to the singing of the Vedas.'

The chief deity in Madurai is the Great Goddess. Her cult was known to the ancient Greeks and an earlier temple is described in Tamil texts of the first century AD. Today none of the fabric predates the Muslim sack of 1314, save the bases of the towers and the walls of the inner shrine to Shiva. But the layout of the city still conforms to the plan required two thousand years ago in ritual texts on city planning: the square of the holy precinct surrounded by concentric circles ('lotus-shaped') of the processional streets, and then the outer walls which were demolished by the British. From a distance the great gate towers rise above the plain marking out the ritual space, a living example of the cosmic city which we shall encounter later in ancient China and Central America; one of the great native Indian cities with ancient roots. In the central shrine the deity stands in the traditional posture of the mother goddess, exemplifying female procreative powers. Her name, Minakshi, and those used for Shiva here, Sundarar and Cokkanathar, come from the oldest

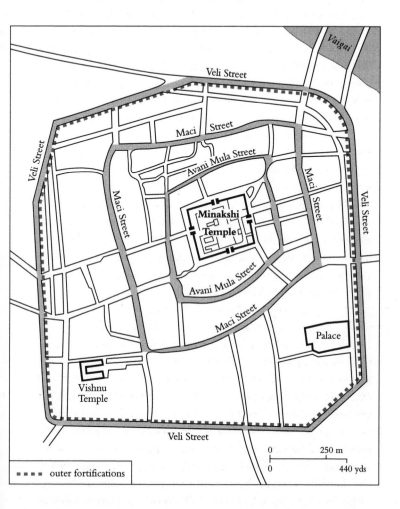

Madurai, a Tamil sacred city. Still a bustling pilgrimage town, attracting 10,000 pilgrims each day, Madurai was known to the ancient Greeks and Romans. The processional streets around the temple are named after the Tamil months; the outer walls were demolished by the British in the 1840s.

stratum of the Dravidian language, and could well have been applied to deities as far back as the Harappan Age.

Once a year the image of the goddess is taken to the banks of the sacred lake to celebrate her marriage to Shiva. This is a ritual as old as civilization; recorded in ancient Babylonia in the third millennium BC, it was still performed there in Hellenistic times. At the lake, she and her consort are garlanded like earthly potentates and serenaded with haunting hymns in Tamil, one of the oldest of the world's classical languages and perhaps a living descendant of the language of the Indus cities. 'The great Goddess,' says an ancient Indian hymn, 'is the cause of all: she is peace, the intelligence in all things, all forms of faith; she is consciousness itself; ever in all things and pervading all creation.' Archaic in name and form, the great goddess of Madurai is part of an ancient and irrepressible current of belief and experience in Indian life which has never been done away with, either by the monotheism of Christianity or Islam, or by the modernization and westernization of our own age; whether it will continue to be so, only time will tell.

THE LAST INVASION: THE COMING OF THE BRITISH

The last great period of Tamil culture was in the seventeenth century. In the north the Moghul empire was showing the first signs of decline. And now the last and perhaps most fateful invasion of India took place. Westerners had coveted India's wealth since Alexander's day. In the eighteenth century competing European powers began to carve out colonies there. Wars between the British and the French ensued in Bengal and in Tamil Nadu, a part of their global confrontation: the great sacred enclosures at Chidambaram and Srirangam were desecrated and used as fortresses by contending foreign armies. Soon India could be depicted as a naked black female, submissively offering her riches to Britannia. And with that India entered the cataclysmic epoch which has left few native cultures of the world intact, the era of colonialism.

The British triumphed because of India's own internal divisions, and because they controlled the sea. Along her coasts they created great ports as the basis of their rule: Calcutta, Madras, Bombay, 'a ring round India.' The early growth of their power in India was under the corrupt and violent auspices of the East India Company. The conquest happened piecemeal and opportunistically with no long-term goal. It was effected at no expense to the British taxpayer, by mercenaries picking off regional threats one by one. Only in 1857 when the great uprising in northern India, the 'Mutiny', put an end to the 258-year existence of the company, did the British government take direct control of its Indian possessions. Ever mindful of tradition, the first viceroy, Lord Canning, read Queen Victoria's proclamation on 1 November 1858 from the rampart of Akbar's fort at Allahabad, by the 'undying tree' and the 'pillar of laws' overlooking the sacred confluence. Thus, following Ashoka, Samudragupta and Akbar, a new *dharma* was announced from the primal place, and India entered a new phase of her history.

Astonishingly, even at the peak of their empire, the British were able to rule one of the most populous regions on earth with just fifty thousand troops and a quarter of a million administrators. The era of British rule, the Raj, has become tinged with nostalgia through the medium of television and Hollywood. But, however we dress it up, imperialism is still imperialism. India was turned into a typical colonial economy, exporting raw material and importing finished goods. The natural resources of India were plundered, and her trees and animals, which Ashoka had protected two thousand years before, were thoughtlessly consumed. And, as has happened all over the world from Africa to native America, the Indians, bearers of the world's oldest living civilization, were treated like children by people who saw themselves as the superior race. In fantastical costumes and invented ceremonies the rulers of a small island five thousand miles away glorified themselves. To them India was the 'jewel in their crown'; for on it depended the very existence of their empire, the greatest ever seen in history. How easy it is to forget that there was an India before the British came which is still there now they have gone.

This is not to deny the complex and profound legacy of the British: above all the English language, but also English ideas of representative government, urban structures, communications, education and secular law, all of which contributed to Indian civilization. Such developments also helped shape the political unity of India: indeed perhaps the very possibility of a single Indian state only arose as a workable idea because the British made it so. Even Hinduism itself would experience reform and revival under the influence of European and Christian ideas. But perhaps the most fateful legacy of the British was to open India irrevocably to a wider world: to force Indians to redefine their age-long civilization in terms of the new secular *dharma* of the West.

INDEPENDENCE

Our search finally brings us back to Allahabad, to the city of the Kumbh Mela, and to the family house of the Nehrus, three generations of whom have ruled India since Independence. In the library here, crammed with books on the European humanist and socialist traditions, Indian democrats met during the 1930s to discuss what India's future path should be. Their hopes and fears have been echoed time and again in our modern world by indigenous peoples seeking to mitigate and learn from the Western impact. How far should the Western model be followed, in terms of industrial capitalism, democracy, Western rationality, Western science? How far can indigenous traditions work as the basis of a modern state? Jawarharlal Nehru, the upper-class, English-educated, first Prime Minister, thought European socialist models were the way forward, and came to believe in a complete break with the archaic traditions of India's past. (At that time, many intellectuals still had faith in the success of the communist experiment in Russia.) In contrast, Nehru's friend Mahatma Gandhi, whose austere bedroom, complete with spinning wheel and floormat, is also preserved in Nehru's house, had faith in

India's own path, in self-cultivation, in local economies and village democracy, in Ashoka's principle of non-violence. For him the greatest legacy any civilization has is simply itself. India's greatness lay precisely in its Indianness, not in a watered-down Western compromise: but the drift of the world was against him. 'The ideals of our civilization,' he said, 'non-violence, equality, pluralism, tolerance – inward and outward – can only become a true force through informed persuasion, not enforcement. Whether the ever increasing multitude of humanity *can ever* develop such theical attitudes I do not know. But I do know that we are committed to it – and that the young are waiting for our support in attempting it.'

The modern state of India was conceived and argued over only seventy years ago in Nehru's house in Allahabad, but it rests on a great tradition extending back thousands of years with an amazing cultural continuity which has continually reasserted itself. In that light the beliefs of the Buddha and Ashoka, Kabir, Akbar and Dara Shukoh can be seen as a living body of ideas of continuing validity, as India pursues its destiny as the most multiracial, multilingual society on earth.

Already the three hundred years of the British period are beginning to feel like a temporary interruption in the continuity of Indian history. The memorials of that era are fading now as a deeper past reasserts itself: the India before the Europeans. And with that past, along with its glories, come the failures and tragedies which civilization is heir to: in India the continuing deep-rooted injustice of caste; the threats of separatism and religious fanaticism; the exploitation of women and the oppression of the tribal peoples; the deep-seated feudalism of some regions which, like caste, has so often defeated the aspirations of Western-style democracy. Such failures, as well as its successes, are rooted deep in India's past.

India has been prodigiously gifted and creative in every field of human endeavour. If we were to choose one characteristic legacy – and it would be a Western choice – then perhaps it is that India placed the spiritual quest at the centre of life in the way that no other civilization did (although India also has an impressive and strong secular tradition extending back as far as the time of Ashoka). From ancient times India defined the goals of civilization very differently from the West. The West raised individualism, materialism, rationality, masculinity as its ideals. The great tradition of India also insisted on non-violence, renunciation, the inner life, the female, as pillars of civilization. And through all the triumphs and disasters of her history, she hung on to that ideal. History is full of empires of the sword. India alone created an empire of the spirit.

EPILOGUE

In the Nehru house in Allahabad a thumbed boyhood copy of the *Gita* still lies at Nehru's bedside, as it always did from his childhood to old age. So perhaps it is still true even at the start of the twenty-first century – true for nations as well as people – that 'we may our ends by our beginnings know'. When Nehru died, according to the instructions of his will, his ashes were scattered at Allahabad at the sacred confluence of the Ganges and Jumna, as Mahatma Gandhi's had been. More recently the ashes of Nehru's murdered daughter Indira and grandson Rajiv were also committed to the turbid waters below Akbar's fortress, with its undying tree and Ashoka's pillar of *dharma*. In his will, Nehru himself had denied any religious significance for the act: 'I have no religious sentiment in the matter. I have been attached to the Ganga and the Jumna rivers in Allahabad since my childhood and, as I have grown older, this attachment has grown. I have watched their varying moods as the seasons changed, and I have often thought of the history and myth and tradition and song and story that have become attached to them through the long ages and become part of their flowing waters. The Ganga especially is the river of India, beloved of her people, round which are intertwined her racial memories, her hopes and fears, her songs of triumph, her victories and her defeats. She has been a symbol of India's age-long culture and civilization, ever-changing, ever-flowing and yet ever the same.'

THREE

CHINA
THE MANDATE
OF HEAVEN

THE DISCOVERY OF THE ORIGINS of Chinese history happened by a strange chance. In 1899 a Chinese scholar in Beijing, Wang Yi Jung, was taken sick with malaria. He had prescriptions for it made up in his local pharmacy. At the time staying with him as a house guest was a friend, the scholar Liu T'ieh-yun (author of the classic novel *Travels of Lao Ts'an*). Liu saw the prescriptions being made up. One of the ingredients was something used by Chinese doctors for hundreds of years, ground-up old tortoise shells, popularly known as dragon bones. To their astonishment, when the two men looked at the bones they saw that on them was a strange archaic form of writing, some of whose characters were the same as those used in modern Chinese writing. Although this ingredient had been used for hundreds of years, this was the first time it had come to the attention of scholars. The two men determined to find out where the bones had come from. They went back to the apothecary's shop and the manager gave them their answer. The bones had been dug up near a dusty little town in Honan province in central China, in the plain of the Yellow River, a town called Anyang. And Anyang would be the key to the rediscovery of the ancient civilization of China.

China was the last of the great civilizations to develop independently in the Old World, well over a thousand years after the first in Iraq. The Chinese way was a vision of life unique to itself: as complete a revelation of 'otherness' as it is possible to find on earth. As one leading western commentator, Simon Leys, has put it: 'It is only when we contemplate China that we can become exactly aware of our own identity and that we begin to perceive which part of our heritage truly pertains to universal humanity, and which part merely reflects Indo-European idiosyncrasies.'

The Chinese conception of civilization differed completely from that of the West and also, in a different way, from that of India too. In China the city began in the Bronze Age not as a centre of population and commerce, but as a ritual enclosure where the king and his diviners mediated between earth and heaven, mankind and nature, living and dead, past and future. And right through Chinese history, from Bronze Age Anyang to the Last Emperor's Beijing, the city retained that character. For the creators of the Chinese tradition, the main goal of human endeavour was a moral order on earth sustained by virtue, ritual, and reverence for ancestors: hence their vision of civilization itself depended first and foremost on these qualities and obligations. And it expressed itself through the idea of harmony, the congruence of opposites, of inner and outer lives, of male and female, light and dark, yin and yang: an elemental balance basic to all Chinese thought, whether in science, philosophy, food or medicine. These ancient ideas permeated all aspects of Chinese life, and were to prove uniquely durable and valuable to the Chinese people. Even the cataclysms of our own time, from the Communist revolution down to the crushing of the democracy movement in Tiananmen Square in 1989, have been played out against these deeper forces which have shaped China for thousands of years, since its beginning on the banks of the Yellow River.

ANYANG: THE BEGINNING OF CHINESE HISTORY

Huang He, the Yellow River, bears its rich yellow silt all the way from Mongolia to the Yellow Sea. It is the destroyer of cities, killer of millions even in our own time. When it leaves the mountains beyond Zheng Zhou, it enters a wide, flat, dusty plain, burning hot in summer. Most of China's Bronze Age cities were

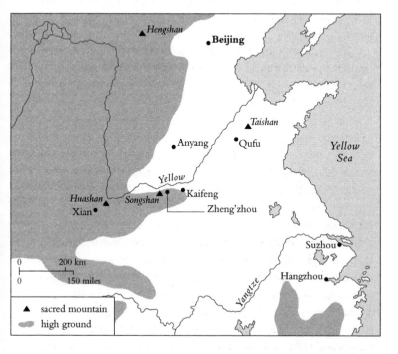

China, showing sites mentioned in the text. The 'middle land' (zhungwo), from which China gets its name, centred on Songshan, the meridian for Chinese astronomers from 1000 BC.

built here, though then the climate was warmer, the land marshier, with sub-tropical flora and fauna. Like the other Old World civilizations, Chinese civilization first arose on the banks of a river, but unlike the civilizations of the ancient Near East, the source of political power did not lie in control of nature, but in control of the past. Whereas in early Iraq or Egypt irrigation was the key to the authority of early kings and states, in China royal power rested on lineage and on divination, the ability to access and co-opt the ancestors.

There is little to see at Anyang today. It is a small pleasant city with Ming dynasty walls and a drum tower. In the old quarter long leafy lanes lined with whitewashed houses lead to two huge water tanks where people walk in the evenings. There is a medieval Buddhist pagoda at whose gates old people still light incense and burn prayers. To get to the site of the Bronze Age palaces where the dragon bones were found you walk out of town a couple of miles through wheat fields to the village of Hsiao-tun. Here, where the Huan river makes a great bend, stood the wooden palaces of Yin, the last city of the ill-fated Shang dynasty.

According to the historian Ssu-ma Chien, writing in the first century BC, the terrible events surrounding the fall of the Shang, a thousand years before his day, took place here. There had been many kings, good and bad, but Chòu was the most wicked and the most intelligent. Strong, lascivious and cruel, he spent his time in orgies, devising dreadful punishments for those of his councillors who complained at his behaviour. Worse, he was negligent to the gods and to the ghosts of the ancestors. Eventually his just ministers turned against him, saying, 'You do not know the mandate of heaven.' And in an action loaded with meaning both practical and symbolic, the 'senior and junior ritualists' deserted with their bronze vessels and musical instruments to the good duke of Chou, who was known to be compassionate and 'to care for the common people.' The wicked Chòu thus lost his access to the ancestors. Then, led by the good duke, Wu Wang, Chòu's enemies closed in on him and attacked him. 'On the day *chia-tzu*,' says Ssu-ma Chien ('when the year star

Jupiter was in the Cancer-Leo station,' adds another tradition with spine-tingling immediacy) Chòu was defeated, 'and he climbed the Deer Platform in his precious jade suit and walked into the fire to his death.' Various traditions suggest the year was 1122 BC, though other dates are possible. The key to the story according to Ssu-ma Chien, and it may be a key clue to the understanding of Chinese history, is that though rulers may be cruel and merciless, through his capricious cruelty and depravity Chòu had lost the mandate of heaven. This conception of a moral order in politics may be a very ancient one indeed.

It was soon clear that thousands of oracle bones had come out of the ground near Hsiao-tun. In 1922, the decade of King Tutankhamun's tomb, Ur of the Chaldees and Mohenjo-Daro, excavations began which would be of no less significance in the history of China, and of the world. Here were the tombs of the last Shang kings and their royal kinsmen and women, packed with wonderful bronze funeral ornaments. Here too was evidence of human sacrifice; for as at Ur in Babylonia, Abydos in Egypt and in Central America, the early Chinese rulers had been buried with the corpses of their faithful retainers. And here too was the answer to the riddle of the dragon bones.

The chemists in Beijing had been grinding up the ritual archive of the Shang Kings. These were oracle bones used by royal diviners to communicate with the ancestral spirits. They came partly from cattle but especially from turtles, the ancient symbol of immortality in Chinese culture. The bones were heated and then split with a sharp implement; the oracles were then interpreted according to the way the cracks ran. Afterwards the bones were annotated with the diviner's comments in answer to questions about birth and death, fertility, sickness, health, even the outcome of royal campaigns, hunting expeditions, and the founding of cities. In these strange marks lay the beginnings of the *I Ching*, the great Chinese book of wisdom, still used throughout the world today. (The beginnings of historiography too, of astronomical and calendrical observations, were 'close to divination and the worship of the spirits' as the ancient historian

Ssu-ma Chien noted.) Here then was a fundamental clue to the origins and early character of Chinese culture, for it was through the magic power of writing that the ancestral spirits could be raised. Indeed, the ancient Chinese word for these symbols – 'wen,' writing – would become the word for civilization itself. In the beginning, in China, was not the city, but the word.

The second key find at Anyang was the bronzes. These exquisite and elaborate ritual vessels were used for sacrifices and ritual meals. Cast by the lost wax process, their extraordinary patterns and detail, their elegance of design and their luxuriant patina have made them among the most coveted of all art objects. Their inscriptions tell of lineage and of the worship of ancestors, basic preoccupations of the Chinese till today. 'Ts'ai Shu, I myself made this,' reads one inscription from the ninth century BC. 'May my sons and grandsons for a myriad years treasure it and use it without limit.' It was the possession of these things, the performance of the correct rituals, the monopoly of bronze and writing which gave the rulers access to the wisdom of the ancestors. This was the basis of political power, and only with this could the ruler possess the greatest of gifts, a gift to be kept only so long as he was just and cared for the people – the mandate of heaven.

Excavations have continued at Anyang. The last big find was the extraordinarily rich tomb of Lady Fu Hao in 1976. And in the last few years Chinese archaeologists have been able to bring to life a whole prehistory which had previously been thought merely legend. Decipherment of the oracle bones has shown that the Shang kings whose names were handed down by tradition were real people. Several of their capitals have been identified; some indeed, like that at the modern industrial city of Zheng Zhou (ancient Ao?) still show great earth ramparts above ground. Tantalizingly, the ancestral ritual centre, the 'Great City Shang' itself has not yet been found, though clues suggest it lies buried in Honan under flood levels by the old course of the Yellow River at a place still called, intriguingly, Shang ch'iu. The discovery in the 1980s of a new Shang city at Yen Shih near Zheng Zhou confirms the impression that these were great enclosures for the performance of royal rituals, 'the pivot of the four quarters,' as later texts put it, ancestors of the imperial enclosures at Xian and of the Forbidden City in Beijing. Inside the walls were the palaces and dwellings of the royal kin. Commoners' houses, bronze and bone workshops and pottery kilns were all outside. Much remains to be understood about Shang society: different clans within the royal lineage may have taken the kingship in rotation, moving the capital each time. But it seems clear that Shang society had two main strata: the ruling warrior nobility (with their ritual specialists) and the village farmers. This division would remain one of the chief characteristics of Chinese society for thousands of years.

Recent excavations have taken the tale back further still. Before the origins of the Shang, legend names a shadowy dynasty called the Hsia. The Hsia were said to have originated near the sacred mountain of Songshan. Here small defended enclosures from around 2000 BC have now been uncovered. This was the very heartland of China, the 'Middle Kingdom', *Zhungwo*, which gave the land its name.

Set beside the long development of prehistoric humankind in China, these new discoveries show that Chinese classical culture was a continuous indigenous development out of a very ancient past. Just like India, its culture was autochthonous, born in its own soil, with a deep-rooted continuity from prehistoric times. This in turn may help explain, as in India, the exceptional tenacity of belief and custom which can be seen throughout Chinese history. The myths have been proved to have a historical kernel. The central concerns of the culture from the earliest times for which there is record were writing, divination, ritual, ancestor worship, history and poetry. The sacred books of classical Chinese civilization reflected these concerns: *Li Chih* (ritual) *Shi Chih* (history) *I Ching* (divination) *Shih Ching* (poetry), books which still provided the ideological basis of the state down to the beginning of the twentieth century, when the empire came to an end.

The civilization of classical China turned these ancient beliefs into one of the greatest achievements of humanity. As with India, it was rooted in the folk culture of the Bronze Age, which lent it an amazing resilience, longevity and distinctiveness. And as in India and ancient Greece, these central concerns and traditions were codified early, in the fifth century BC, codified in a way which defined the path China would take. And their codifier was Kung Fu Tzu – Confucius.

CONFUCIUS: SHAPER OF THE TRADITION

Today graves are dug again in the cemetery of the Kung family in Qufu, Shandung province, their gaily coloured paper decorations fluttering in the wind. Extending over 500 acres, containing 2500 years of ancestors, this unique place was vandalized in the Cultural Revolution, the bones of the dead dug up and execrated in a futile attempt to exorcise the continuing power of their spirits. But today it is still a monument to the most influential figure in Chinese history, and to those who have faithfully conserved his legacy.

It was Confucius who transformed the magic of the Bronze Age into the conception of the state as a moral order sustained by virtue and ritual. Confucius lived in that astonishing Axis Age when the Buddha was alive, as were Pythagoras, the Greek philosophers, and the Jewish prophets. He was not a religious leader, but the codifier of China's traditions in history, poetry and ritual. His teachings were the ideal of Chinese government for two thousand years, and even though (like the Buddha and Jesus) we only have his reported sayings, what has come down to us is an unmistakable and individual voice.

At the centre of Confucius' message was a simple and original idea. He was not concerned with God or the afterlife or heaven. 'I don't know anything about those things,' he said. His concern was that of every government today: how to build a just and stable society here on earth. And his answer was this: goodness, moral virtue, was the essential quality needed to keep society together. *Jen*, humanity, was the most valued goal to which we can all aspire as citizens.

People are not born good, Confucius thought, they need to

be taught goodness – both rulers and ruled. It was essential that the rulers were taught goodness, spiritual and intellectual, because if rulers rule with unjust harshness and severity, meting out excessive punishments and oppressing the people (like the wicked Chòu), then people lose their faith in the law, they lose their respect for themselves, they have no sense of shame. But if people are taught goodness and self-respect, then they have all those qualities and they regulate themselves. Confucius' vision then was of a moral society bound together by mutual respect and trust. And though an aristocrat, his was in a sense an anti-authoritarian idea because the control of the ideology would rest with the scholars, not with the emperors who themselves had to obey that golden mean or risk forfeiting the mandate of heaven, as even today's rulers of China have found out.

The seriousness with which these ideas were followed by China's best rulers is shown by a passage in the last testament of the K'ang-hsi emperor composed in the winter of 1717:

The rulers of the past all took reverence for Heaven's laws and reverence for their ancestors as the fundamental way in ruling the country. To be sincere in reverence for Heaven and ancestors entails the following: be kind to men from afar and keep the able ones near, nourish the people, think of the profit of all as being the real profit and the mind of the whole country as being the real mind, be considerate to officials and act as a father to the people, protect the state before danger comes and govern well before there is any disturbance, be always diligent and always careful, and maintain the balance between leniency and strictness, between principle and expediency, so that long-range plans can be made for the country. That's all there is to it.

Confucius' golden rule of personal virtue sounds very old-fashioned today, as too does his emphasis on ritual. But of course it is still true today that personal virtue is the basis of civilization. As for ritual, it gives definition to relationships; it expresses respect; it gives form to the link with the ancestors which all humans seek. 'Without rituals,' said Confucius, 'we may as well be dead.' But in the end he thought it all depended on goodness: if we are not good, what use are rituals? And here's the rub: what *is* goodness? What *is* a good person? Confucius' pupils were given a simple answer. 'He who loves others,' said the master. 'The good person wishing to stand himself helps others to stand; wishing himself to arrive, helps others arrive. The ability to see the parallel to your own case is the secret of goodness.'

In Qufu today on Confucius' birthday, grand ceremonies take place once again, sponsored by the state. In the last few years the rulers of China have revived a number of the old Confucian traditions, at least in their outward form. Performance of such rituals ceased after the Communist revolution; indeed, as a state cult they ended with the Republic in 1911. Today they are done by actors and the ceremonies in Confucius' home town are for tourists: largely foreign Chinese tourists from Taiwan, Hong Kong and Singapore, rediscovering roots severed, temporarily it would now seem, in 1949. It is a vision of a splendid past which the rulers of China in our time attempted to do away with, in the belief that new traditions could replace them. But just when we think we have shaken it off, the past has an uncanny habit of coming back to restate its old claims on our loyalties. 'Appreciate the past,' said the master, 'and understand the present. Only then can you learn virtue and goodness.'

TAOISM: THE WAY

Long before Confucius, the ancient Chinese believed that earth, nature and the cosmos were part of a harmonious natural order, the Tao, the way or path. The search for the right path, Taoism, is the second great stream of Chinese thought; a natural mysticism to set beside the practical common sense of Confucius. The early Taoist classics, such as the *Tao te Ching* and Chuang Tzu indeed look like reactions against Confucian civil morality, and what they saw as the artificial and restrictive structures of society. But Taoism came to be seen not as an alternative, but as the other half of a necessary balance in life. Indeed it was said that the complete person was a Confucian by day (in public life) and a Taoist by night (in private).

The pilgrim path up the sacred mountain Taishan is a symbol for that search for the Tao. It is the easternmost of the five sacred mountains which define the heartland of Zhungwo, the Middle Kingdom. Taishan has been sacred since prehistory. It has been walked for thousands of years by Chinese people, rich and poor, from Confucius and the first Emperor to Chairman Mao. And today tourists and pilgrims are coming again.

The ascent of Taishan prompts questions about the way the great eastern civilizations have viewed humanity's place in the natural world, and the divergence of traditional eastern and western conceptions of spirituality. For so long western culture has seen nature in terms of control and exploitation. But for the ancient Chinese it was the source of all harmony and balance. They thought it was our duty as human beings, through art, religion and science, to understand the harmony: not to abuse it or needlessly to change it, but to go with the force of nature, the yin and yang as they would say.

All the way up the mountain paths on Taishan there are shrines to the traditional deities of the land. Smashed during the Cultural Revolution, they have been rebuilt and people are once more stopping to light incense, make prayers and leave offerings. The little Taoist temple on the top of Taishan, dedicated to the Goddess of the mountain, was wrecked by the Red Guards in the Cultural Revolution. It is now lived in again, not by actors but by real Taoist monks and nuns who came back in 1985, committing themselves to the old way. In 1990, with the help of a government grant, they reroofed the main shrine. All over China, with freedom of worship again allowed, such acts of restitution, of reclamation of the past, are taking place. How they will fare it is too early to say. 'In the end,' said the Taoist sage Lao-Tzu, 'all creatures return to their distinctive roots, that is called returning to one's destiny. It is knowledge of what is constant which is true wisdom. Woe to him who wilfully innovates and ignores the constant.'

From the top of Taishan is a wonderful vista: to the west the Yellow River plain; to the east the Yellow Sea; all around great wooded precipices and fairy-tale crags crowned with little pagodas; below, the path makes its dizzying descent to the foot of the mountain, and the immense Sung temple, the Tai Miao. On the summit the pilgrims wait for the first glimpse of the dawn, as the great did before them. It was up here that Chairman Mao proclaimed 'The East is Red,' but that was before his Great Leap Forward turned the dawn yellow with pollution. Over two thousand years ago the first emperor; Chin Shi Huangdi, surveyed his kingdom from here as the sun rose and announced, 'Now I have united the whole world.' Confucius said simply, 'Now I realize how small the world is.'

THE UNIFICATION OF CHINA

China was unified in 221 BC by Chin Shi Huangdi, after centuries of warfare among the Yellow River states. The ideology of the Chin emperor's rule came from the legalists, who rejected Confucian morality on the grounds that a state could only be governed by a ruthless system of law applied to all. The tension between these two conceptions of government still continues.

The Chin emperor standardized the Chinese script and weights and measures; he built a massive canal system still visible north of Xian in Shaanxi province, and the earliest Great Wall to keep out northern nomads. But his rule was remembered with fear and bitterness for a thousand years. Most reviled by posterity was the burning of books: a systematic attempt to confine written knowledge within the imperial library and allow access only to practical subjects such as drugs, medicine, oracles, agriculture and forestry. Any critical or heterodox literature was burned. The Chin emperor's special wrath was reserved for history. 'Fearing the power of the past to discredit the present,' he buried the historians alive with their books, even exhuming and execrating the dead. By this, it was hoped, only one version of the past might survive.

Towards the end of his life, Shi Huangdi's megalomania led him on a search for everlasting life, climbing Taishan to drink the ambrosia of dawn from magic bowls on the summit. Outside Xian he built an immense tomb guarded by an army of life-size terracotta warriors, a sensational discovery when excavated in 1974. Inside the tomb was a stone labyrinth with pits and blind alleys and crossbows set to fire automatically if disturbed. In the central chamber the ceiling represented the sky with pearls for stars; on the floor was a stone map of the world with the hundred rivers of the Empire flowing mechanically with mercury. Buried with the king were his childless wives and concubines, and all the craftsmen who knew the secrets of its construction. Whether the tomb was opened and looted, in the rebellion which followed the emperor's death is unknown: it may still hide some of its secrets.

The Chin emperor failed in his attempt to rewrite Chinese history. In the first century BC the great Ssu-ma Chien was able accurately to reconstruct many of the pre-Chin traditions and chronology, beginning what is perhaps the world's richest and longest continuous historiographical tradition. But the spell cast by the first emperor would remain on China's rulers, right down to the 'last emperor' Mao and his successors, whose revolution was in some senses just that: a complete circle going back to Shi Huangdi and his fear of history and its power to give meaning to the present.

FIRST CONTACTS WITH THE WEST

The Silk Route in the Gobi Desert, in the far west of China, is one of the most inhospitable landscapes in the world. Across this desert from the second century AD came the ideas, goods and people which ushered in China's first international age. China had never been wholly immune to influences from the west, even in prehistory. But the desert, the Himalayas and the great massif of the Tibetan plateau were a great obstacle to close and regular contacts. And so, more than any other Old World civilization, China had developed in relative isolation, uniquely itself; neither wanting nor needing anything from the outside world. But now contacts opened up with central Asia, Persia, even Rome, and especially with India. For what the Chinese were looking for was not material riches but spiritual enlightenment: the wisdom of the Buddha.

Today the evidence of that great meeting of civilizations is to be seen all over western China: in the ruined Buddhist monasteries along the Silk Route, for example, and especially in the thousand Buddhist caves at Dunhuang with their exquisite paintings. Right down the Yellow River, into the heartland of the Empire, vast monumental carvings and elaborate cave shrines and monasteries are still to be seen, such as the Longmen caves outside the old capital of Luoyang. But what was the appeal of this foreign religion, that it exercised such a hold on the Chinese imagination? A down-to-earth, practical people, the Chinese never developed, and perhaps never needed, an elaborate theology of their own. Indeed the Western idea of a personal God is utterly foreign to them. But Buddhism, with its atheistic and democratic message, its deep care for ritual, was to have the greatest appeal of all the foreign religions which took root here (until, and perhaps including, Marxism). Buddhism was the third great stream making up the current of Chinese civilization, a spiritual discipline to set beside Confucian wisdom and Taoist mysticism. The later Chinese came to believe that these three philosophies contained the essential ideas of civilization and without any one of them life would be unbalanced; that however sophisticated and technologically advanced a society might become, its people could only be fulfilled through inner enlightenment and the contemplation of eternity. It is a dilemma which lies at the core of civilization.

In the Tang dynasty (618–907 AD) intrepid Chinese scholars went on great missionary journeys through Tibet to India, to bring back authentic texts and relics of the Buddha. In a little temple in a secluded valley outside Xian are kept the ashes of the most famous of those missionaries, Hsuan Tsang. Some of the texts Hsuan Tsang brought back from India in the seventh century AD are still here: palm leaf manuscripts written in Pali, the old language used by Buddhist scholars in Ceylon. Perhaps Hsuan Tsang bought them during his stay in Kanchi, the great South Indian centre of scholarship: fragments of 650 books which he and his helpers brought back to Xian for translation. A stele in the monastic library shows him, rucksack on his back, a lamp to light his way, doggedly braving the elements to bring home his precious cargo. It is rare in history that we can pin-point the very moment when one great civilization goes out to learn from another. In the contemporary biographies of Hsuan Tsang, and other missionaries of that period, we can still feel the overwhelming excitement they experienced in encountering 'the other' in India. Theirs was a curiously moving and open-minded sensibility: as the Emperor declared in 638 to a group of Nestorian Christians applying for his permission to begin building their church in Xian, 'This teaching is helpful to all creatures, and beneficial to all mankind, so let it have free course through the empire.'

XIAN: 'AXIS OF THE WORLD'

In the eighth century AD all roads in Asia led to Xian or Chang'an, as it was then known. One of the greatest cities in the world, rivalled only by Baghdad and Constantinople, its vast square was laid out 'like a chess board' as the poet Tu Fu said: a huge ritual enclosure with a central boulevard four miles long and twice as wide as today's avenue which leads to the city's bell-tower. The present city walls – seven miles of them – were built in Ming times; you have to go out into the farm fields north of Xian to find the earthworks, platforms, and isolated pagodas from the earlier Han and Tang cities. But walk under the Ming drum tower at sunset when all the street vendors are out, and enter the winding streets of the medieval Muslim quarter which surround the beautiful Friday Mosque. Then you will get a sense of what life must have been like in the Tang city. This was the first time that foreigners had entered China in any numbers and, as often in later days, they were supervised by the authorities and confined to their own area at night, well away from the centre of power. Over in the western quarter of the Tang city, in the foreigners' enclave, you could find an anarchic vitality and a sophistication and cultural mix that impressed all visitors to Chang'an. Here there were Muslims, Christians and Jews from Syria and Iraq, Zoroastrians and Manichaeans from Iran and Central Asia. There were Persian conjurors, Turkish money-lenders and Hindu fakirs. In the cafés there was central Asian music, Asian food (as there still is today) and also entertainment from singing and dancing girls from Persia and even further afield – some of them it was said with blonde hair and blue eyes! Small wonder then, that as a poet of the time, Tu Mu, said, 'You could misspend your youth in cities like this and end up with nothing but the reputation of a wanderer in the blue houses.'

In Chinese eyes, the Tang dynasty was above all the most golden of the many golden ages of their poetry, an art inseparable from that of calligraphy, and whose roots must go back to the shamanistic magic of the Bronze Age. For the Chinese indeed, composing poetry was one of the essential ingredients of civilization. And if we could choose a single career to symbolize this first international era of Chinese culture, then it would be perhaps the great poet Li Bai, or Li Po as we know him in the West (650–701). Li Po was a product of the Silk Route. He was born not in China but in central Asia and spoke one of the Turkish languages. He spent his early years as a wandering soldier of fortune; one of his greatest poems is about the futility of war, 'A cursed thing which the wise man uses only if he must.' Then he found his opportunities in Chang'an, in the greatest city on earth. His personality was magnetic, irascible, self-taught, with flashing eyes, a fearsome voice and a heaven-sent talent. He was a prodigious drinker too: the story goes that he died, falling drunk into a river, trying to catch at the reflection of the moon! Li Po wandered through the music halls and the cabarets and restaurants of Chang'an and the other cities of China, his ear tuned not only to classical poetry, but to folk songs and ballads and the latest pop music coming hot out of central Asia on the caravan trails. He refused pointedly to sit the Confucian examinations, preferring to

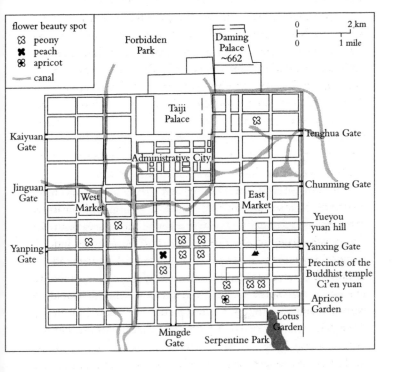

flower beauty spot
- 🕸 peony
- ✖ peach
- 🕸 apricot
- canal

Forbidden Park

Daming Palace ~662

Taiji Palace

Administrative City

Kaiyuan Gate

Tenghua Gate

Jinguan Gate

Chunming Gate

West Market

East Market

Yueyou yuan hill

Yanping Gate

Yanxing Gate

Precincts of the Buddhist temple Ci'en yuan

Apricot Garden

Lotus Garden

Mingde Gate

Serpentine Park

Xian in the early eighth century BC, showing the beauty spots: the Chinese vision of the city. There were over a hundred Buddhist temples here, along with four Zoroastrian shrines, two Christian churches and a mosque.

do it, as he would have put it, his way. Always an outsider, but still today, along with his friend Tu Fu, among the Chinese people he is their best loved and best known poet.

'All pomp and circumstance,' said Li Po, 'all wealth and power is like clouds passing by.' The great Tang poets, like the best artists of any time, understood suffering, they felt for the poor and saw through the pretensions of the rich. They were familiar with the lifestyle of the royal family, whose tombs still lie outside Xian guarded by their spirit ways, their ceremonial avenues of the dead. Inside their tombs we can still come face to face with the people of whom the poets spoke: Tang princes and princesses who lost the mandate of heaven when their dynasty subsided into famine, disorder and chaos. On one wall young courtiers play polo, a game imported along with their expensive horses down the Silk Route from Central Asia, 'proud and cocksure, thinking that all under heaven was theirs to sport with, that their power would be everlasting.' In Princess Yongtai's tomb are women who were perhaps imperial concubines like those described by Li Po: 'On marble stairs behind crystal blinds, fretting as they grow old, trapped by their wealth, their tears leaving damp stains on their silk slippers.'

In the last days of the Tang, in the mid-eighth century, the writing was on the wall: an incompetent government could no longer feed its people. 'Beyond the vermilion gates and the smell of wine and flesh,' wrote Tu Fu, 'people are freezing and starving to death. In thousands of villages they harvest only weeds, while the women do the ploughing. The people of China can face any test if only their leaders treat them humanely.'

THE SUNG GOLDEN AGE

Amidst famine and internecine struggle, the Tang dynasty ended in social upheaval and revolution, like many in Chinese history. But it was followed by one even greater. Four hundred miles from Xian eastwards down the Yellow River lies Kaifeng. In the eleventh century AD Kaifeng was the capital of what is regarded as the peak of Chinese civilization, the Sung dynasty (960–1279 AD), a cultural golden age to set beside any in world history. Kaifeng was a new kind of city in Chinese history: a commercial centre with manufacturing industries – metalwork, porcelain and textiles (as it still is today). It was a cheek-by-jowl place jammed with restaurants, its skyline smoking from coal-fired furnaces. Something of a backwater now, the old city of Kaifeng has escaped the wholesale modernization many cities suffered under the communists. Its narrow alleys are still full of balconied shops from the Ching dynasty, and in its warren of streets you can still find signs of the many foreign communities who settled here in the Sung period, in time becoming Chinese. Kaifeng's first Christian church was built then, and it is still a cathedral city today. One lane is still known as the 'alley of the sect who teach the scriptures,' that is, of the Jews. Their synagogue closed a century ago, the farthest outpost of Judaism. There are still a few Chinese Jewish families there today, with the mezuzah on the door frame, and the candelabrum in the living room. Near the alley is a lovely old Islamic mosque, with a fine wooden pillared prayer hall. Like the Jews, the Kaifeng Muslims came as traders from the Near East in Sung times, whether from Persia or South India they are no longer sure. Today their community, fifty thousand strong, is mainly poor shopkeepers and small traders: a living survival of the great cosmopolitan era of medieval Kaifeng.

In the Sung period many of the great inventions were developed by which we live our lives today. Cast iron technology was so advanced that entire segmented bridges and pagodas could be built, which still stand today. Deep drilling for salt and natural gas was commonplace. In Kaifeng they built a huge mechanical clock and were able to measure the year to within twenty-six seconds of what can be done today. Another great invention which came into its own at this time was printing. Printing had come out of the age-old Chinese tradition of making stamped prints on paper: the first printed book is dated 868. In the Sung period, dictionaries, scientific works, star charts, paper money, even newspapers followed; they also experimented with movable type. This was almost certainly the most literate society which had yet existed on earth; the aristocratic and exclusive cast of Chinese culture was broadened and given fresh vitality as material of a more general appeal was made available in print. In this intellectual climate, the Sung Age produced a series of brilliant figures aspiring to the Confucian ideal of the 'Renaissance man': statesman, scholar, poet, painter and philosopher. Some, like the Statesman Ou-yang Hsiu (1007–72) and the philosopher Chu Hsi (1130–1200) it has been said, 'stand comparison with the greatest human spirits of all times and places.' They were humanists in the true sense of the word. They believed in the innate goodness of humanity, and in the possibility that through rational inquiry and lived experience, human beings could find the single immutable principle of all things. Ou-yang Hsiu has also left us some delightful personal sketches which convey a vivid flavour of his time. One story tells of his boyhood in an uncultured town, and the finding of a tattered old book from the Tang dynasty in a neighbour's waste paper basket. Taking it home the boy found its writing 'rich and profound, forceful and erudite,' though its style was then out of fashion: 'I was still young and could not understand it all, but I *did* see its spirit was grand and overpowering.' And so his future path opened up! Later, his *Sound of Autumn* reads like a fragment of a Chinese *Remembrance of Things Past*. Finally there is a delightful retirement tale of the old drunkard carousing with his friends in the Chu mountains, frying wild vegetables, drinking wine and playing chess. 'An old man now, white-haired, garrulous, but relaxed and at ease with himself – and already half kettled. Who is this drunken old buffer? Why Ou-yang Hsiu of Luling!'

Another great Sung figure was the historian Ssu-ma Kuang. Working in Kaifeng and then Luoyang between 1064 and 1085, he produced a *Comprehensive Mirror* of Chinese history in 360 fascicles, with an appended 'examination of differences' making explicit his selection and criticism of sources. This was a vision of history in the Confucian moralist tradition, 'to understand the merits and demerits of past ages, and to serve as models and warnings.' How extraordinary it is that we still sometimes hear the claim that the West's is the only true historiographical tradition in the world!

The Sung achievement was right across the board from industry and technology to landscape painting, literature, poetry, and history. It appears now as one of the great cultural epochs of the world, the rival of Abbasid Baghdad and classical Athens; and with the existence of printing they could disseminate their ideals across Eastern Asia. Sung thinkers like Chu Hsi reshaped the old ideals of Confucian philosophy, of inward cultivation, self-development, and secular piety; they harnessed them to an examination system which ensured that only the best could aspire to positions of power and they made that the root of their state culture. This philosophy would dominate Eastern Asia for the next millennium, and is the cultural basis of the phenomenal success of countries like Japan and Korea in modern times, for they are still essentially neo-Confucian.

'THE GREATEST CIVILIZATION IN THE WORLD'

Kaifeng fell to northern invaders in 1126, and for over a century China was divided, with the southern Sung continuing to rule from Hangchow. But between 1259 and 1279 the Mongols, who had shattered Iran and Iraq far to the west, overcame China. It was a crucial moment in Chinese history, as crucial perhaps as the Communist takeover in 1949. Their traditional civilization was put to the severest test of its resilience. The Mongols were alien to settled city civilization, to Chinese institutions, to Confucian values. Rather like Roman scholars in Western barbarian courts, Chinese statesmen had to persuade their new overlords of the worth of the tradition, and to work to perpetuate it by inculcating the Mongols with Sung values.

It was this task which prompted the historian Ma Tuanlin (1254–1325) to compose his *Comprehensive Survey of Written Records and Traditions* – a monumental encyclopaedia in 348 chapters attempting to transmit the essence of the heritage though a strikingly modern perception of historical continuity through institutions. 'These are what determines continuity, not mere events, the saga of rise and fall, order and chaos, and in our time this is where historians should turn their attention.' Whether such an integrative venture would be possible now, in the late twentieth century, is an open question. But in the thirteenth and fourteenth centuries, continuity was in fact assured, and the Mongol period, the Yuan (1279–1368), as it turned out, was another great epoch of Chinese art and culture; moreover its economy was still the richest in the world. In the thirteenth century when European visitors came in numbers to China for the first time, they were open-mouthed at what they saw. Sailing up the Grand Canal in Suzhou, the Venetian Marco Polo had no doubt that this was the greatest civilization in the world. 'I tell you,' he said, 'in all truth, the riches and resources, it's all on such a stupendous scale you wouldn't believe it unless you saw it. If the Chinese were warlike they could conquer the rest of the world. Thank goodness they're not.'

At this time agricultural and commercial revolutions led to a population boom in the south which saw China become the most populous country on earth, as it still is today. But the country was self-sufficient and could feed all its people. In 1344 the Arab traveller Ibn Battuta travelled for sixty days up the Grand Canal passing through the most ordered, fertile and productive landscape he had seen in all his travels from the Atlantic seaboard of North Africa to the South China Sea. Even the ordinary peasantry, he thought, enjoyed incomparably the highest standard of living in the world.

There perhaps comes a point in the life of any civilization when the basic necessities of life for the people have been satisfied; food, shelter, freedom from violence. Then it can aspire to extend its higher ideals to more and more of its people. The key conception of Chinese civilization had always been the search for harmony, and all its manifestations were part of that search, from the patterns of the bronze caster and the painter, to the designs of the porcelain maker and the silk weaver. By cultivating such arts, the noble person could realize the universal harmony which Confucian wisdom sought. For the Chinese this was the supreme mission of civilization: it was an élite vision, to be sure; but no less impressive for that.

The path to such wisdom still began with the magic of writing. From its beginnings as a tool of divination, writing remained the means of access to the wisdom of the ancestors. The symbol for writing, the sign called 'wen,' had begun by signifying the characters on the oracle bones. Through time its meanings deepened and widened, to embrace writing, culture, refinement, elegance, till the sign 'wen' coupled with the sign 'ming' (light or brightness) came to mean civilization itself. It was nothing less than an expression of the way the Chinese saw the world.

MARVELLOUS VISIONS FROM THE STARRY RAFT

But now the way China saw the world began to change. Above a vast silted bay at Quenzhou in south China, which was once the busiest port in the world, stands a Muslim shrine and the graves of three followers of the Prophet, who first brought Islam to China in the late seventh century. In the shrine a stone stele records that Ming dynasty admiral Zheng He, a Muslim, prayed here before he embarked on one of seven great voyages of exploration in the fifteenth century; voyages which could have easily changed the course of history.

Zheng He's huge ships dwarfed anything constructed in the fifteenth century West: 500 feet long, weighing 1500 tons, with watertight compartments, and a stern rudder 30 feet high. They sailed by magnetic compass bearings, with paper charts. Zheng He was the last in a series of great Chinese navigators who as early as the Tang period had sent expeditions to plot the meridian arc from Vietnam to Mongolia, and to map the stars from Java to within twenty degrees of the south celestial pole. Unlike the western admirals who came after him, Zheng He had not come to conquer, though he claimed suzerainty over all overseas Chinese. He sailed his fleets to the great south Indian harbour of

Cochin, long the meeting place of East and West. En route, on the northern tip of Ceylon, he left a trilingual inscription affirming he came in peace, and offering respects to the gods of three religions, Allah, Buddha, and Vishnu. In Cochin, Zheng He would have seen the Chinese fishing nets imported in Mongol times. For South Indian merchants had long traded with China, exchanging pepper and spices for porcelain and silk. From Cochin, Zheng He explored East Africa, where Chinese pottery has been found as far south as Mozambique. He visited the Persian Gulf and went on pilgrimage to Mecca itself, writing down its description in his log. He could have 'discovered' the West had he had the inclination! It would be nearly a century before Vasco da Gama sailed into the same harbour of Cochin from the West, not as a bearer of peace but a harbinger of war and conquest.

Then suddenly the imperial bureaucrats of the Ming dynasty banned any further voyages, despite their rich commercial potential. The ships were broken up and their log books destroyed, leaving us only the fragmentary accounts in later Chinese historians, 'marvellous visions from the starry raft' as one of them described the great adventure. Now only a few stone inscriptions on the wind-swept hillside at Quenzhou remain as clues to one of history's unsolved mysteries: why were the voyages stopped?

Western thinkers have always taken a typically simple line on the stopping of Zheng He's explorations. For them it would be like calling a halt to manned space exploration on the eve of the first moon landing. Even now the ban is seen as proof that the Chinese were backward-looking and rigid in their thought; that they had no desire for new knowledge and were run by a class of hidebound bureaucrats whose world view was closed. Proof too, it is said, that the West was the fount of science and technology and progress; that the West had a monopoly on the spirit of enterprise. But, as always in history, there are many ways of looking at the same question. After all, as we have seen, it was the Chinese who were the great technological innovators. They had made virtually all the key inventions on which the later hegemony of the West would depend. So perhaps it really comes down to the question of how different civilizations think we should *use* technology. And perhaps then the Chinese saw, quite sensibly on the face of it, that their true interests lay inside their own borders, cultivating their soil, and cultivating the inner life; searching for the harmony that had always been the goal of their civilization. And perhaps it was the West on the other hand which had a compulsive desire to change; a compulsive need to invade other people's space, both moral and physical; and a refusal to accept limits on its own.

Since the eighteenth century, it has been customary for Europeans to talk about the East needing to 'catch up' with the West. These days that is obviously happening all around us in a material sense, if it has not happened already. But it takes two to make a dialogue, and perhaps the West still has some catching up to do. Perhaps the West still has to learn from the East a way of cultivating its inner space; of accepting limits on desires and space in an increasingly finite world. At the beginning of this modern dialogue between the East and the West the French philosopher Pascal said that the trouble with Western man was this, that he did not know 'how to be content in an empty room.'

The banning of the Ming voyages was, nevertheless, part of a deepening introspection in Chinese culture. Now behind a new Great Wall to keep out the barbarians, the Ming government based itself in a capital far to the north: Beijing, the 'North City,' which had been founded by the Mongols in the thirteenth century. From here they waged interminable strength-sapping wars against the Mongols and other steppe peoples who continued to threaten their northern border throughout the fifteenth century. At home, in administration as in culture, they became increasingly rigid in doctrine and practice, imposing an all-pervasive literary censorship, and were unremittingly harsh in their legalistic enforcement of punishment. Meanwhile at the Altar of Heaven in Beijing the Emperor continued to perform the rituals of the Bronze Age in the belief that the world would never change.

THE WAY IS QUESTIONED

Elsewhere the world was changing fast. In the sixteenth century western missionaries and scholars came to reside in Beijing for the first time, propounding new views about the world, time and the cosmos. In 1602 the Jesuit Matteo Ricci could present the Ming court with a world map showing undreamed-of continents. The brilliant cartographical achievements of the Sung were now superseded. From this time the longest and richest intellectual tradition in the world increasingly seems to turn in on itself. Though the cultural achievements of the seventeenth and eighteenth centuries were still extraordinary in their diversity, the state-sponsored scholarship, on which the whole edifice depended, reads more and more like a dialogue with the past. In the national library in Beijing is the most pointed proof both of its greatness and of its progressive desiccation. Here is the greatest literary enterprise of all time, an encyclopedia running to 79,000 hand-written volumes, the *Ssu-Ku-Ch'uan-shu*. Still in its original shelves and boxes, beautifully tooled and varnished, labelled in green, red, blue and grey according to the Imperial cataloguing system of Spring, Summer, Autumn and Winter (for Classics, History, Philosophy and Literature), it is a testimony to the idea that all knowledge, past, present and future, could be contained in a single room. This was the most ambitious of a number of huge encyclopaedic projects and dictionaries commissioned during the seventeenth and eighteenth centuries by the Ching dynasty which succeeded the Ming in the 1640s. Among them too was a comprehensive collection of Tang poetry containing nearly 50,000 poems. Such works are a testimony to the intellectual culture of their time, a culture refined and often brilliant still in literature and art, for a long time competent in administration too; but slow to react to the way the world beyond its horizons was changing, inquisitorial towards critical opinion, and more and more bogged down by the vast and bureaucratic feudal order bequeathed to them by the ancestors.

The most successful of the Ching rulers, K'ang-hsi, was one

of the greatest and longest-lived of all Chinese emperors, and has left us one of the most touching of all ruler autobiographies ('I'm now approaching seventy. The country is more or less at peace and the world is at peace. Even if we haven't improved all manners and customs, and made all the people prosperous and happy, yet I have worked with unceasing diligence...'). By any standards, his was another brilliant epoch. So, too was the equally long reign of the Ch'ien-lung emperor (1736–96). But all this time, western explorers, missionaries and condottieri were spreading their power and influence across the globe. And so too, far away in 'barbarian' Europe, Bacon, Newton and Descartes had been concerning themselves not with how to perfect the past, but how to control the future. And now some Chinese intellectuals began to plead for a more open approach to knowledge, among them an obscure young historian called Chang Hsüeh Cheng, who has been compared to the greatest historians of the past, to Ibn Khaldun or Thucydides.

Born in 1738, Chang Hsüeh Cheng lived on the very eve of the most momentous upheaval in Chinese history since the time of the Chin Emperor nearly two thousand years before; in other words, the clash with the West and the changes that would engender. It was he who attempted to reappraise the way that the Chinese had seen history since the very beginnings of the Confucian tradition. For him, history was an all-embracing concept which would include the entire canon of Chinese literature. The Confucian classics, he said, were 'all history.' Confucius may be a true guide to life but he is also simply a historical text. And the time was past, he thought, when history should be merely minute textual analysis and compilation by teams of scholars, burrowing away on a rigid and old-fashioned curriculum. History should be dynamic and meaningful. Some have seen Chang Hsüeh Cheng as a precursor of the revolution, a prophet of democracy, an enemy of feudalism. No doubt that is an exaggeration. But in 1799, two years before his death, he wrote a prophetic letter about what he saw as the now inevitable decline of the Ching dynasty and the worrying future prospects for

China. This was a time, he said, when history should no longer concern itself merely with the past but 'should use the past to reform the present,' and, indeed, to look into the future. The historian's greatest gifts, he said, are not just knowledge but inspiration and insight. An historian's inspiration, he thought, could be compared to the *I Ching*, the Book of Changes, in that it too enabled him to look into the future. At the moment of Chang's death, China was about to come face-to-face with another culture, whose view of history was diametrically opposed to that of the Chinese tradition. The Europeans with their Judaeo-Christian heritage believed that history was purposive, that it was leading towards an appointed end – and that they would be the winners.

THE CLASH WITH THE WEST

Had China been left to solve its own problems, its faltering economy, its growing poverty and social injustice, its feudal class structures and its rigid educational system, it might have moved into the modern world spared the suffering it was to undergo. But it was not. The first Chinese descriptions of Westerners are not flattering. 'These barbarians have a grim look, untidy hair, an unpleasant smell. They have no rituals worthy of the name. They are liars and are rather arrogant. They conquer countries by fraud and force, ingratiating themselves in a friendly way before they oppress the natives. At the heart of their conduct is violence.' Such were early Chinese reports of the Spanish in the Philippines. They were not to change their opinions.

By the eighteenth century the coasts of the south China sea were frequented by the Spanish, the Dutch, Portuguese, English and later Americans. They all came bearing Chinese inventions: gunpowder, the stern rudder, the magnetic compass, paper maps; coming not just to sell but to impose their goods, their ideas, their religion, their will. They soon set up trading colonies, paid for by the illicit trade in goods like opium. In the tale of colonial infamy this is one of the least known episodes in the West, but it culminated in what might be seen as the pivotal event of nineteenth-century Chinese history, the Opium War.

For the British, the point of the opium trade was simply to sell opium to China. In practice this meant getting as many Chinese people addicted to the drug as possible. But opium was prohibited in China, and hitherto had an almost negligible local consumption. So it had to be sold illicitly from the one permitted trading post on the mainland, Canton, and from off-shore bases like Gulangjou island. The indispensable link in this set-up was India. There, the British imperial possessions had grown in the last decades of the eighteenth century. The British themselves produced nothing which the Chinese wished to buy, but in India they could grow opium and, to a lesser extent, cotton, which could be traded for the luxuries which the British desired, especially tea, which by then had become a national obsession. And so an infernal triangle was set up between Britain, China and India which parallels the tragic triangle of the previous century between Africa, the Caribbean and Europe, the slave trade. And this was no small business. Incredibly in the early nineteenth century opium was the biggest single trade anywhere in the world.

In 1839 when the Chinese government attempted to put a stop to the opium trade, the British responded with force in a manner which has never been forgotten in China. In what Gladstone called 'the most disreputable war ever fought by the British,' the Chinese fleets, hopelessly outgunned and outdated, were smashed to pieces, defeated by the very technology which they had invented but allowed to stand still. For the Chinese, defeat was a shattering revelation. They were forced to watch impotent as the Western 'barbarians', their cultural inferiors, began to carve up the Middle Kingdom into colonies with the same greedy relish that they would scramble for Africa and dismember India. The Opium War was a watershed in Chinese history. They had resisted the Westerners for over two centuries: now the 'foreign devils' had become bound up with the very future survival of the Middle Kingdom. Soon China was shaken by a series of tremendous blows: the milleniary rebellion of the Taiping, defeat in a war with Japan, and the failed Boxer rising.

It was a time of tremendous intellectual ferment, as the old self-confidence ebbed away. Reformers analysed all too well the reasons for the West's success – technology, energy, intellect – much as they deprecated it. Many felt that 'within a hundred years China will adopt all the West's methods,' as Wang Ta'o wrote in 1870. The example of Japan beckoned, adopting the ways of the West without letting its people onto Japanese soil. Other reformers, like the charismatic Kang Yu Wei, called for an end to the empire, and for freedom and equality of race, sex and colour through a regeneration of the Confucian way itself! Meantime, unable to cope with the pressure of the outside world, the Chinese imperial government finally collapsed. A Republican movement had arisen in the nineteenth century, long before the founding of the Communist party, but the imperial government had been almost malevolently resistant to all change. The abolition of the Empire after 2100 years and the establishment of a Republic in 1911, came too late to solve China's intractable problems: an impoverished peasantry, underdeveloped industry and the continued presence of the colonial powers. 'The great time of revolution' had arrived as the *I Ching*, the Book of Changes, states. And the great man was at hand in whom all belief would reside: Mao Tse Tung. In the 1930s a bitter civil war broke out between communists and nationalists. The Japanese invasion of 1936 turned Mao's communists into a national liberation front. Eventually in 1949, Mao and the communists took power on a heady tide of emotion and optimism, after years of civil war, famine and foreign rule.

But in their haste to erase the past, the communists killed millions by ill-judged reforms and tyrannical violence. The so-called 'Great Leap Forward' in the 1950s brought about catastrophic famine in the countryside with untold damage both to the environment and to the social fabric. The 'Cultural Revolution' of the 1960s proved more damaging to China's heritage than the Mongols ever were. The promise of open debate in the 'Thousand Flowers and Thousand Schools' evaporated into brutalized and stagnated intellectual life scarring the next generations. And all this was in the name of a Western ideology and a Western conception of history! Only now, as the dust settles after one of the most extraordinary and significant episodes in the history of the world, can we as outsiders begin to detect the lineaments of the older China – spiritual, psychological, social – still in place, which Mao, like the Chin emperor, sought to obliterate in his illusory quest for a world freed from the weight of the past. For without the past, as Confucius said, what are we?

THE LEGACY OF CHINA

Today the Chinese people are living through a time of great opportunity. Though they are still without political power, their country has become an economic giant, with nearly a quarter of the world's population. Over the past twenty years the Chinese Communist party has shed its Marxist ideology and is now an authoritarian bureaucracy with uncanny resemblances to those of imperial times. And the future? One of the older generation of republicans, Liang Shu-ming, writing in the 1920s, boldly prophesied that the future world civilization would be reconstructed Chinese civilization! Though admiring of some Western values, such as individual freedom and our scientific traditions, which he hoped China might someday embrace in synthesis with its own humanistic values, Liang condemned wholesale imitation of the West as a false path. Western market democracy in particular he thought at odds with Chinese tradition: 'The fundamental spirit of China was to seek harmony and synthesis, that of the West to go forward to change: a path which has been destructive of nature, and of the spirit.' What the West would in time come to need he believed, was Confucian *jen*: humanity. Such hopes now seem misplaced.

China's contribution towards the history of humanity has been enormous. Its political system brought peace and stability for long periods to a large proportion of the population of the world: no mean achievement even today. The government may often have been harsh and autocratic, but by a thousand years ago they had developed sophisticated examinations for the selection of officials on merit which were unparalleled elsewhere till our own time. In science and technology they were far ahead of the rest of the world until the modern era. The Chinese were perhaps the finest craftsmen of any civilization; in bronzes, silk, jade, porcelain and lacquer. Their matchless calligraphy and painting are another side of their sensibility. Their literature too is full of wonderful achievements, especially in poetry. Theirs was also the earliest and longest tradition of historiography. But of all their legacies, perhaps their greatest was also the most characteristic: the ideal of harmony and reconciliation of opposites propounded by the Taoists, coupled with the Confucian vision of practical morality. At the root of their civilization lay the shamanistic culture of the Bronze Age with its reverence for the ancestors, for virtue and for the magic of writing. So deeply ingrained were these conceptions that in spite of all the vicissitudes of Chinese history, their civilization was able to regenerate itself without ever breaking the cultural continuity right down to the end of the empire and the communist revolution. After the terrible traumas of the twentieth century, it is not yet clear how the next renewal will come about, or whether it will draw on the past for its models as so often before. Whether Mao and his followers have indeed severed the link with the great tradition of classical China, it is, as he liked to say, too early to tell.

But of one thing we may be tolerably sure. In the *I Ching*, the ancient Chinese book of divination, there is a hexagram entitled 'Revolution.' 'In a revolution,' it says, 'two mistakes must be avoided. You must not move with excessive haste nor use excessive ruthlessness against the people. What is done must correspond to a higher truth. A revolution not founded on inner truth will come to grief; for in the end the people will support only what they feel in their hearts to be just.' That, as Confucius would have said, is the meaning of the mandate of heaven.

FOUR

EGYPT

THE HABIT OF CIVILIZATION

IN THE VALLEY OF THE NILE, the ancient Egyptians created one of the earliest, most magnificent and long-lasting of the world's civilizations. The images of the 'great tradition' of Pharaonic Egypt are so familiar to us today – pyramids, obelisks, sphinxes, hieroglyphs and so on – that it is easy to forget the immense vistas of time which separate us from them: time which also constitutes Egyptian history, a history as rich and interesting as the Age of the Pharaohs. There were nearly a thousand years of Greek, Roman and Byzantine rule in Egypt and over 1,300 years have passed since the coming of Islam. The 'break' with the ancient world (if for a moment we may speak in such simplistic terms) occurred a long time ago. And it is there that we begin our story, at the point of the break: at the beginning of the end, with an account of Egypt written in Greek by a native priest called Manetho.

THE END OF A TRADITION

Alexander the Great's conquest of Egypt in 332 BC marks a truly profound caesura in its history. We say this with hindsight, of course. There had been such breaks before; in the 108-year rule of the Hyksos for example in the seventeenth century BC. More recently Assyrians and Persians had held sway. But none had disrupted the extraordinary continuity of institutions and customs; what one modern scholar in a memorable phrase called Egypt's 'airless immobility.' But Alexander's triumph would be far more threatening to the old country, exposing its introverted ways of seeing to the dynamic culture of international Hellenism, to new ways of construing nature, society and politics. Never again would a native Pharaoh rule the 'two lands', after three thousand years of recorded history. As we see it now it was indeed the beginning of the end of an old Egyptian world which had shown such amazing resilience, in ideology, in religious belief, and in institutions, for so long. Nearly a thousand years of rule by Greeks and Romans would see the transformation of the native culture, the end of the old state structures, its priesthood, its writing system, its language, its cults, the gods themselves. But despite this, such times of crisis in history open up new directions, new possibilities, and the Hellenistic age would see the transmission of Egypt's legacy through the ancient world as the Greeks went native in 'the land of ancient wisdom.'

Not long after the Greek conquest, an ethnological literature began to emerge, mostly written by Greeks living in Egypt, but also by travellers, aimed at a Greek reading public who had been fascinated by things Egyptian since the famous travel book by Herodotus in the fifth century BC. The Greeks believed Egypt to be the place where religious cult was first organized on earth, a land of inconceivable antiquity. We can get a sense of how they looked up to the older culture in the words which Plato puts into the mouth of an Egyptian priest: 'O Solon, you Greeks are never anything but children; there is not an old man among you.' Their insatiable curiosity for Egypt is brought out in the story Heliodorus tells of an Egyptian priest visiting Delphi surrounded by a crowd of Greeks 'plying me with all kinds of questions. How do we worship our country's gods? Why do we worship animals? What do our different cults mean? How were the pyramids built? What about the underground labyrinths? In short, on every aspect of our customs, for there is nothing a Greek likes better than listening to tales about Egypt.'

Much of the new literature after Alexander's day was based for the first time on first-hand testimony from Egyptian priests: we might compare this with those British scholars in India of the eighteenth and nineteenth centuries, who first elucidated Hindu ritual and Sanskrit texts with the help of Brahmins. Under the Greek ruler Ptolemy II (282–246 BC) a programme was begun to translate Egyptian (and Jewish and Babylonian) books into Greek, and it was in his day, probably soon after 280 BC, that an Egyptian priest called Manetho wrote his *Aegyptiaka* (Matters of Egypt) which, as it turned out, would be one of the key documents in the modern reconstruction of ancient Egyptian history.

Manetho may have been born when Alexander was still alive. He came from Sebennytus in the Delta, which is now a small country town off the Damietta branch of the Nile, surrounded by palm groves and cotton fields. Close by was a great temple to Isis, the 'Compassionate Mother', which was beautifully embellished in Manetho's day by Ptolemy II. (Now ruined, its sacred tank is still visited by women to pray for children.) If we try to imagine ourselves back in the Egypt of Manetho's day, the first thing to strike us would have been an overwhelming sense of living in an old country, and in a holy land. The Delta was full of ancient towns, some still inhabited today. Twenty miles to the south-west of Sebennytos was the great cult centre of Amun Re, now called Tanta, where even today more than a million people go to the Delta festivals of Seyed el Bedawi at the vernal equinox and at the summer solstice during the rising of the Nile. Then fakirs and dervishes perform before rapt crowds, serpent swallowers and snake charmers ply their trade, and musicians and poets give impassioned recitals of religious and folk stories. A little further to the south-east, at Bubastis, was the biggest popular festival in the Hellenistic age, where according to Herodotus, 700,000 people descended each year for a riotous religious carnival. All the way up the Nile from the Delta to Thebes in Upper Egypt, and even beyond, the journey was marked by similar cult centres of great antiquity, many of which were rebuilt under the Greek dynasty who could easily identify the native gods with their own. There was Min at Akhmim (Pan), Hathor at Denderah (Aphrodite), Horus at Edfu (Apollo); there were the great gods at Thebes, which the Greeks called Diospolis (literally 'God town') and the shrines which studded the river bank past Esna and Kom Ombo as far as the first cataract and the baking orange cliffs of Nubia. Only perhaps in India, on the Ganges or the Cauvery, could one find something of a similar sensibility today: a holy land with a sacred geography where every day's journey is marked by great temples and pilgrimage places.

Manetho became a priest at Heliopolis, the greatest priestly centre in lower Egypt, near today's Cairo. We know that he wrote books on Egyptian religion; a description of the main festivals; a study of ancient ritual; a short text on the making of *Kyphi*, an ancient concoction which was used in incense and medicine; and a treatise on theories of Nature. He was no great thinker; the significance of his work is that he wrote in Greek. He was probably the first Egyptian to write about his country for foreigners. That he wrote when he did is no coincidence. He was clearly not setting out to satisfy colonial curiosity, or the demands of tourism. Rather, he was making accessible local ideologies, beliefs and history to the Greek rulers of Egypt in their own language, trying in the process to convince them of the value of traditional Egyptian culture. We know for example that he criticized the 'ignorance' of Herodotus on Egyptian history, whom he saw as dealing in tourist guide fictions. Manetho was also perhaps consciously moving his own priestly class into the bilingual world of Hellenism: a strategy of survival which has its parallels elsewhere in this book, in Muslim India, Mongol China, and Spanish Central America. Notorious for their resistance to any foreign customs, the Egyptian 'Brahmins' now had to move with the times or perish.

Manetho's work divided Egyptian history into thirty dynasties, stretching back nearly three thousand years before his own time, to a founder with the enigmatic name of Menes, which may mean 'the accomplisher' or 'the bringer together'. Menes, it was believed, had united the two lands of Upper and Lower Egypt and formed a single unified state. Manetho was able to give the exact length of his reign and those of his seven successors in the first dynasty. As an Egyptian speaker, versed in

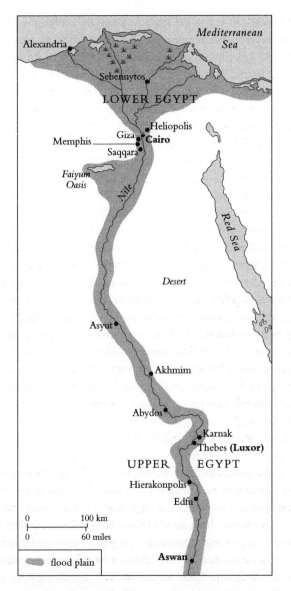

Egypt's unique geography has shaped the character of its people and their civilization till today. Only the modern damming of the River Nile at Aswan threatens to disrupt its extraordinary continuity of ecology and culture.

hieroglyphic writing, Manetho still had access to the priestly traditions at important temples like Heliopolis. Such shrines each had their library room, the 'House of Life,' an example of which survives in the Ptolemaic temple at Edfu, with the catalogue of its sacred books still engraved on its walls. From these books Manetho provided details of Egyptian religious traditions and ritual. Other sources provided him with his chronological framework. Still surviving fragments such as the Turin Papyrus and the Palermo Stone show that in his day records existed not only from as far back as Menes, but of the kings of the separate kingdoms of Upper and Lower Egypt even *before* the unification.

Manetho's text has not survived: we know it through extensive quotations of it by Roman historians and Church Fathers in the first millennium AD. The framework of Egyptian history it offered though, influenced subsequent historiography down to the Arab period. It was as we see it now, a bridge to a future world, the world which succeeded the ancients. For the great tradition of Egypt, unlike those of India and China, did not survive into the modern world, but lost its identity, submerged in the great changes which swept the Near East between Hellenism and Islam. The Greeks were the last to see it as it was, and though Manetho could not know it, his work was a requiem for a world which, even as he wrote, had almost passed.

BEGINNINGS

'The Egyptian Nile,' said the great Arab traveller Ibn Battuta, 'surpasses all the rivers of the world in sweetness of taste, in length of course and utility. No other river in the world can show such a continuous series of towns and villages along its banks, nor a basin so intensely cultivated.' The civilization of Egypt, like those of Iraq, India and China, drew its life from a river. Like the Ganges in India, the Nile was worshipped as a divine force itself; as the giver of life. There are liturgies to the river from the second millenium BC; Byzantine Christian hymns; a Syriac prayer from the twelfth century AD. The Coptic feast of St Michael still marks the rising of the river on 17 June each year, on the 'Night of the Drop' which, tradition says, falls from heaven to begin the rise: a tear of Isis according to the ancients. Though these age-old customs are breaking down today, responses and blessings are still performed, too, in traditional Muslim households: 'May Allah pour the Nile abundantly over the whole land.' This then was a river like no other, and it made a country like no other; running for six hundred miles between dunes and cliffs, the narrow ribbon of blue water and green fields on average only six miles wide. Egypt's geography shaped the very character of its civilization and its people. Where the spirit of Iraq was pessimistic, here when the Nile flooded each year, as the ancients said, 'the fields laugh, men's faces light up and God rejoices in his heart.' From the life-renewing soil left by the inundation, the Egyptians drew a cheerful confidence in humanity, in the permanence and stability of things. In striking contrast to ancient Mesopotamia, theirs was always an optimistic civilization.

Strong natural frontiers; a rich agricultural soil produced by the annual flooding; tremendous mineral resources in stone and precious metals: all this was the very opposite of early Iraq. It generated a magical self-confidence and a unique cultural purity for over three thousand years of Egyptian history. Modern archaeology has pushed back the horizons of Egypt's prehistory and shown that many of its later traits can be found in the deep past of farming in the Nile valley. Farming villages appear in the flood plain in the sixth millennium BC, cultivating wheat and barley and domesticating sheep and goats. During the next two millennia we see the gradual formation of several tiny kingdoms along the valley, and in the Delta, the two regions which still present the fundamental divide in Egyptian history, culture and geography. After 4000 BC there is a substantial increase in population and size of settlements; developed crafts and technological skills are in evidence, working in stone, bronze, copper, slate. The first small towns, walled in mudbrick, appear by 3500 BC, with the rich tombs of local dynasties. Our evidence from the Delta is scanty. Most of the early sites in that area are deep in silt, so we have to rely on a group of sites from Upper Egypt to conjecture what happened next.

In the mid-fourth millennium BC, Upper Egypt seems to have been divided between three kingdoms, centring on Nekhen (Hierakonpolis), Nagada and This. Very likely they were rivals. Hierakonpolis was the cult centre of the hawk god Horus, and Nagada of the god Seth. One of the great mythological themes in Egyptian religion was the conflict of Horus and Seth, the sons of Osiris, the king of the dead. Many scholars now believe these myths dimly reflect a real struggle between the two kingdoms which preceded the conquest of the Delta by the 'Horus Kings'.

HIERAKONPOLIS: THE BEGINNINGS OF EGYPTIAN HISTORY

Central to all these questions, indeed to the whole story of the uniting of Egypt, are the remarkable excavations which took place at Hierakonpolis in 1897–8. Today it is an obscure little village fifty miles upstream from Luxor; its name Kom el-Ahmar, 'the red mound.' Here was the centre of the prehistoric tribal kingdom of Nekhen, the shrine of a local divinity called Horus, the hawk. Hence its Greek name, which literally means 'hawk town.' In 1897 two British archaeologists, James Quibell and F. W. Green, came here looking for the origins of Egypt, at a time when the archaeologists of the European colonial powers were uncovering imperial origins elsewhere, at Mycenae, Boghaz Köy, Babylon, Nineveh and Assur. Hierakonpolis had been an insignificant place in later Pharaonic Egypt: there were fragmentary remains of a New Kingdom town here with mudbrick walls. But Quibell and Green were looking for clues from earlier still. For Egyptian royal tradition always insisted that this place had been the cult centre of the kings who united Egypt; indeed right till the end of Pharaonic Egypt its name would still retain an honorific precedence among the royal titles. In a field beyond the village, they made a thrilling discovery. Underneath the later Horus temple they found a heap of ceremonial palettes, ivories

122

and maceheads from the ritual stores of Egypt's first kings, kings with totemic names like Cobra, Catfish, Scorpion, Hawk; kings who inhabited a glittering, barbaric world very different from that of the historical pharaohs.

Among the finds was perhaps the most significant single object ever dug up in Egypt: a slab of black slate two feet long, cut with scenes commemorating the deeds of a king called Narmer. Central to the palette is an image clearly meant to convey the conquest of the Delta by a king of Upper Egypt; indeed perhaps it is the very moment of Narmer's triumph. Wearing the crown of Upper Egypt, he dashes out the brains of the captive King of the Delta, symbolized by a papyrus clump. Headless enemies lie in rows before the standards of Horus the hawk. On a stone macehead, the same king Narmer is shown receiving an important female personage from the North. This may possibly represent a royal marriage, legitimizing his new position in the Delta. Other palettes showed the destruction of hostile towns by armed gods of Upper Egypt, symbolized by their totems, the lion, the scorpion, and the hawk. On a great ceremonial macehead a king called Scorpion cuts an irrigation ditch with a mattock, one of the primal acts of kingship; around him standards depicting Seth and the phallic god Min are associated with the hawk standard of Horus. In some sense then, the archaeologists had found a ritual deposit of some of the earliest kings of Egypt, possibly even of the unifier himself. But was Narmer the same ruler as the shadowy Menes?

A year later Green returned to make another intriguing find in the same area. He uncovered the remains of a large circular mound of clean white sand about 150 feet across and 8 feet high, enclosed by a sloping sandstone revetment. There were signs of a walkway leading to some central feature. Green thought the dating was late prehistoric, perhaps even before the first kings of dynastic Egypt. He interpreted the mound as being a symbolic representation of the mound of creation itself; the first island which had risen out of the seas of chaos at the beginning of time and on which the first life had landed, the hawk: this he argued was the ritual centre of the Horus kings who had founded Egypt.

Since his day, parallels have been discovered for such manmade cult representations of the primordial place, in Teotihuacan in Mexico, at Cuzco in Peru, and especially at Eridu in Iraq, which enjoyed comparable symbolic status in Sumerian religion and royal mythology. As we have seen, a natural island at the confluence of the Ganges and Jumna rivers was the focus of similar beliefs in ancient India. We are dealing with a universal myth. And in fact when an American expedition re-excavated the site at Kom el-Ahmar in 1967, they were able to identify all the features Green found, and to add the crucial detail which was missing. In the centre of the mound had been a small hut-shrine of reed and mud, surrounded by a reed fence, a kind of structure which can be seen everywhere in the Upper Egyptian countryside still today. Inside, no doubt, had been the cult statue of the divine hawk, and various objects, some of which perhaps had been the ceremonial palettes and maceheads found in 1897. Here then was the symbolic centre of the Horus kingship of Nekhen which preceded the double crown of Upper and Lower Egypt. The mystery of Menes, though, was and is still unsolved. Whether the king on the Narmer palette is the same man we cannot still be certain. The find of jar sealings at Abydos coupling the two names was once thought to have proved their identities beyond doubt but this may not be the case. Narmer indeed may have been Menes' predecessor by a generation or two. The enigmatic names of the pre-Dynastic beings on the Palermo Stone – Seka, Khaya, Neheb, Mekh and the rest, are still a mystery too. But we now know a lot more about the prehistory of Egypt's first towns, where some of these kings may have ruled. The settlement at Hierakonpolis has been traced back to 4500 BC; those at Nagada and Abydos to 4000 BC (the former was an important town from 3500 BC). This suggests a whole prehistory is still waiting to be recovered for the centuries preceding the triumph of Menes, the unifying of Egypt around 3100 BC. The ultimate success of the First Dynasty kings after Menes may have been, as Manetho painted it, the victory of a family from Abydos.

But they never forgot their debt to their shadowy predecessors from Hierakonpolis, whose archaic mound shrine was kept unaltered well into the Pyramid Age. Theirs was the story of local kings, clans and lineages, local gods, cults and totems being transformed into national ideologies. Out of such prehistoric tribal struggles, the 'great tradition' emerged: the first true state in the world. The ideological basis of prehistoric kingship, its symbols and myths, proved uniquely long-lasting, indeed it lay at the heart of Egyptian civilization. The divine Kingship of Horus would survive for as long as ancient Egypt itself.

Not far from Kom el-Ahmar, in the great temple at Edfu, that same creation myth would be expounded in loving detail for colonial Greek overlords nearly three millennia after Menes' death. Edfu was commenced after Alexander the Great's conquest of Egypt, beginning in 237 BC. It was built for the Greek overlords, with minute attention to the traditional Egyptian iconography and sacred architecture. On its walls we learn that every Egyptian temple was a symbolic representation of the original mound of creation, with the simple reed shrine surrounding the perch on which the hawk had landed. And no matter how big the temples became in later ages, the Holy of Holies was still that simple reed shrine. In the inner sanctum at Edfu the polished stone shrine still remains, gleaming in the half-light. Carved on its inner walls, the visitor can still see the line of reeds surrounding the space where the image of the hawk was kept. A whole theory of society was bound up with this myth. For the temple was not only a depiction of the first place, but of the first time, the time when the pattern of a stable society was handed down to humankind; a pattern to be maintained by kingship, law, religion and ritual, and which, it was believed, would suffice for eternity as long as the rituals were correctly performed. The universe then, and civil society, were conceived of as static. Progress, change, new questions, new answers were simply not needed. And indeed they would not be needed until Alexander the Great conquered Egypt three millennia later.

So in the predynastic period, the time leading up to Menes,

the time when 'Scorpion' the 'Fighting Hawk' ruled 'the followers of Horus' at Hierakonpolis, we can see the development of many of the mainstays of later Egypt: efficient farming, metal-working, centrally organized irrigation, pottery, stone-working, ceremonial and monumental architecture, elaborate burials, long-distance trade. The oldest gods are already there in the palettes, labels and sculpture from Nekhen, Abydos and Coptos: hawk-headed Horus, Min from Akhmim and Coptos the wolf god, the vulture goddess, Anubis the jackal god of the dead, Thoth the moon god, the patron of writing, Ptah. Here are familiar forms of worship, the aura of divine kingship, the funerary beliefs and customs, the distinctive artistic styles. These lineaments lasted over three thousand years; they can still be traced into the Muslim period, and in certain cases – for instance the ritual laments and libations, folk medicine, burial rites, birth prayers, seasonal festivals, and even the belief in the *ka* or double (forbidden by the Koran) – have survived till today.

For the Egyptians then, divine kingship was the guarantee of a stable cosmos. It is an idea which can be traced across the world from Shang China to Aztec Mexico. And at Abydos those first kings of Egypt were buried with immense brick mortuary temples, their elaborate brick façades imitating those of earthly palaces. For a period, the First and Second Dynasty kings practised human sacrifice, burying royal wives and retainers in the tomb, as was done in Ur of the Chaldees and Anyang, and in classical India, where the practice of Sati, the immolation of royal wives, was only stopped in the nineteenth century. But human sacrifice was rapidly abandoned in Egypt; indeed it went against the grain of the whole of Egyptian culture. The tombs at Abydos were massive brick rectangles with a labyrinth of supply rooms packed with treasures and stores for the afterlife. In 1991 the sensational find here of no less than five full-sized boat burials, three hundred years earlier than the Khufu boat at Giza, shows the extent of this provision for life after death. And so the key themes of Egyptian history were laid down very early; centralized power, royal rituals and the cult of the dead intertwined to form the ideology of the world's first state.

THE PYRAMID AGE

Moving northwards along the Nile, the narrow valley meets the green expanse of the Delta. At this strategic point, close by today's capital, Cairo, Menes built his royal city Memphis. Early dynastic Memphis is now buried beneath many feet of river silt, but on the sandstone escarpment above the flood plain are the royal cemeteries of Memphis, the great funeral complex of the Third Dynasty kings. At Saqqara the mudbrick architecture of Abydos was turned into stone: the world's first large-scale stone architecture. The necropolis at Saqqara extends for miles, and was still being embellished in Greek times. But the central feature is a huge ceremonial complex constructed in around 2700 BC for King Zoser. A vast ritual parade-ground was laid out for the reception of tributes and performances of jubilee ceremonies renewing the king's rule. A series of side chapels enshrined the deities of Nekhen, Nagada and the other upper Egyptian cities. Overshadowing the whole area was a new innovation, a gigantic stepped tomb, 200 feet high: the first of the pyramids. This idea of Zoser and his architect Imhotep (who was later deified) caught on in an extraordinary fashion. In a handful of generations around 2500 BC, a series of gifted Kings, Huni, Senefru, Khufu, Khafre, building bigger and bigger as each seemed to try to outdo his predecessor, created the greatest series of funeral monuments the world has ever seen.

There are many myths surrounding the building of the pyramids. The Hollywood biblical epic version had slave gangs, whipped along by tyrannical masters. But though slavery existed in ancient Egypt, this was not a slave society; that is, the mass of the workforce was not enslaved. The pyramids were built by free or semi-free peasants. In fact in a long reign it was perfectly possible for a government to mobilize huge-scale state employment to build such monuments using the workforce in the wet season when the Nile flood left idle hands.

The Egyptian word for a pyramid means 'a place of ascension' and in this light perhaps we should compare the pyramid to the artificial mountains built by other cultures, for instance the Babylonians, Maya, Moche and Aztec. All civilizations of course have sought validation for their power over the masses by creating great public symbols. And what more awe-inspiring demonstration could there be of the real power of kings who could command such memorials? But clearly they are more than simply an early example of totalitarian architecture. Scholars now believe that in the Egyptian pyramid the dead king becomes a manifestation of the Sun God himself. In the step pyramid at Saqqara we can see the transitional stage in this idea: a staircase on which the king's spirit could ascend to heaven and then go back to his tomb. In the same way the ziggurat at Sippar in Babylonia, for example, could be called 'the stairway to bright heaven.' The true pyramid is simply an extension of that idea. It is both an image of the rays of the Sun God coming down to earth and a celestial ramp for the ascension of the soul: a typical piece of Egyptian imagination, in which an immaterial concept is represented in such material form. And on winter days in Giza, it is often possible to see the sun breaking through the clouds and shining down at the same angle as the pyramids: a stairway to heaven, formed by the rays of the sun on which the king, 'nimble and wise, could ascend to the indestructible stars.'

THE PATTERN OF EGYPTIAN HISTORY

It is not our purpose to summarize the whole of Egyptian history here, even if that were possible. Our concern is the character of civilization and its 'great tradition', and the momentous transformations which eroded that character under the Greeks, the Christians, and the Muslims. For much of its ancient history Egypt remained extraordinarily stable for long periods, with no fundamental change in the ideologies and beliefs which made up the 'great tradition': typified perhaps, to the modern eye, in the unchanging style of its art. The Old Kingdom (c.2700–2100 BC) whose zenith was the Pyramid Age, was a time of tremendous royal power as we have seen, and it saw a big increase in population from an estimated half million in the pre-Dynastic period to two or three million in the time of Khufu. This placed great reliance on maximizing the use of the land flooded and fertilized each year by the inundations. Around 2200–2100 BC the same prolonged dry period which caused such problems for the Ur III kings in Iraq brought a series of consistently low floods and precipitated half a century of famine. This helped pull a declining old order apart. The monarchy was overthrown, and for a period Egypt went back to being two lands, as it had been a thousand years before. But the norms and values of Egyptian civilization were so deeply rooted and enduring that within a century, centralized royal power was restored and a new era of peace and prosperity ensued.

Again, the impetus came from the south. During the interregnum after the Old Kingdom, a small independent kingdom had grown up around the town of Thebes in Upper Egypt, which now enters Egyptian history for the first time. The Theban Mentuhotep restored the unity of the two lands in 2130 BC and the Theban tradition tended to view him as a second founder comparable to Menes. Thebes itself became the southern 'capital' which it remains to this day: testimony to the deep-seated sense of identity existing in Upper Egypt. Mentuhotep and his kin built tombs and a memorial temple to which the image of their patron god Amun was carried by boat in a splendid procession each year: the beginnings of a festival which still takes place today. Through the Middle Kingdom (1991–1786 BC) and the New Kingdom (1587–1085 BC) the once small country town of Thebes was adorned with a series of gigantic shrines and, along the great bowl of western cliffs across the river from the town, a series of huge mortuary temples: the most spectacular assemblage of monuments in the ancient world, a vast city of the dead. Known to the Greeks as 'God town', its fame carried down to Homer, who speaks of 'hundred-gated Thebes'.

There is no evidence in this long period that people seriously considered alternative forms of government to that of rule by a divine king: indeed evidence for revolts against the Pharaonic state is virtually non-existent (unlike the Greek,

Roman and early Islamic periods which were constantly shaken by social uprisings). In modern terms theirs was a provider state, providing a basic standard of living to all its people through control of the resources of the Nile. In return, enormous surpluses could be spent by the rulers on tombs, temples and palaces. Through these great buildings the state expressed its ideologies of power: its belief in the indivisibility of divine and earthly rule, and in the need for a stable cosmos. Such ideas may have been essential requisites for the creation of civilization at the start, and yet, even today, almost all of us still live in nation states with some or all of those same characteristics. Our thinking is still shaped by their religious and social myths, and especially by the myth of the Great Ruler, King or God.

In the New Kingdom the state seems to have developed into a more pluralistic society, rather than the simple hierarchy we imagine in the Pyramid Age, where everyone knew his place. There was still the massive state apparatus, the priesthood and the bureaucrats whose job was to articulate the state myth handed down from Menes. But it was flexible enough to adapt to a form of rule which in the New Kingdom we would recognize as essentially political. One of the intriguing results of recent research has been to show how the development of professional institutions – army, civil service, ministries, priesthood – led in the end to the day-to-day life of the state being taken over by those who dealt in economic realities. The king was still the divine figurehead but he had much less real power. The world had changed from the sublime theocratic unity of Khufu: it had become a self-directed polity held together by customary rights and obligations which had evolved over an immense period of time, incorporating regional groups, local traditions and immemorial predilections.

The fact that in the long history of Pharaonic Egypt there seem to have been few attempts to overthrow the existing order suggests that the state was on the whole successful in managing the rural community on which it rested. Without a system of money at the local level, it needed an elaborate and sometimes pettifogging system of redistribution of surpluses to sustain the huge élite and all the service sector. It was patriarchal and to a degree authoritarian. But in that it is not so far from many Near Eastern countries today, especially the traditional landowning classes. But the arbitrariness had to be matched by responsibility. And so it was at the top too. God, as king, had consented to guide the nation. Society had a pledge that the unpredictable forces of nature would be well disposed and bring prosperity and peace, which generally they did, for three thousand years. Nor did the Egyptian view lack ethical content, for truth and justice were 'what the gods live by' and were an essential element in the established order. As the great Egyptologist Henri Frankfort said, 'Pharaoh was not in our sense a tyrant, nor was his service slavery.'

DECLINE

The first millennium BC saw periods of prosperity but long periods of foreign rule, from the Assyrian attacks of the eighth century to the Persian conquest of 525. During the seventh century for a brief time Egypt was still a first-rank power in the Near East, but from then on its life as an independent state was as a second-rate force struggling to preserve its autonomy against more ruthless and powerful oriental neighbours, with whose military prowess they could not compete. Egypt now entered a 'stark decline' as one modern scholar has put it, enduring two periods of domination under the Persian empire. Gradually its rulers responded to the new military technology, employing Greek mercenaries and commanders, adapting their adminis-tration and making halting steps towards a money economy. But there was no fundamental change: the overall impression is of continuity of ancient practice with no question of a radical restructuring of Egypt's institutions. Indeed there was much harking back to the great days of the Old Kingdom in the art and architecture of the time. In that sense, rather like early nineteenth-century China, however successful and enduring, their state was now stuck in the past, surrounded by powerful neighbours who were no longer organized as theocratic states. Perhaps the greatest change though was the idea that the king was no longer divine; no longer the repository of righteousness, truth and justice, or the ally of the gods. The first millennium BC was a time of great brutality and upheaval across the Near East, and it may be that the ideological basis of Egyptian civilization was already undermined before it fell to the Greeks in the fourth century BC.

GREEK EGYPT: ALIENS IN AN ANCIENT LAND

In 332 BC Egypt was conquered by Alexander the Great, and then Egyptian civilization turned away from its immemorial roots towards the sea and a wider world. For thousands of years far back in time even before the days of a United Kingdom of Egypt, the Egyptians had looked no further for their contacts than Arabia and the Red Sea, Nubia in Africa, Syria and Palestine. But now with the Greek conquest and the founding of Alexandria, a shift in the centre of gravity of Egyptian history took place. For the next thousand years they would find themselves part of a Greek-speaking Mediterranean world. This signalled the beginning of the end of traditional ancient Egyptian culture: it was gradually transmuted by the dynamic internationalizing culture of the Hellenistic age which extended as far as central Asia and formed one of the important foundations of the later Islamic world.

In these changes Alexandria was a great catalyst. In the first century BC a Roman author could write that 'Alexandria is without doubt the first city of the civilized world, in size, in elegance, in riches and in luxury.' 'It's paradise here,' said the poet Herodas. 'You can get anything you want – money, shows, games, women, wine, boys, the best library in the world, in short all earthly delights.' Like twenties New York, Hellenistic Alexandria was a land of opportunities whose streets were paved with gold. It drew immigrants of all kinds; bankers, clerks, engineers, poets, even religious drop-outs, whose lives have been rescued from oblivion by the extraordinary wealth of archive material from papyrus dumps at sites such as Oxyrhynchus. Here was the Macedonian recluse Ptolemaios who was so moved by the Egyptian religion that he went native, rather like a Western Hare Krishna devotee in India, serving the rest of his life in the temple of the Serapeion in Memphis; or Dryton the Greek cavalry officer who married a local girl and whose family in the next generation were already beginning to lose their Greek identity. Their tales were symptomatic: Greeks could go native, learn the local language and assimilate; but Egyptians were much less willing to give up their customs, and for most of the period the Greeks still remained aliens in a foreign land. This is not to say that the cultures did not meet. In the catacombs of Alexandria the visitor can still enter the weird and wonderful world where Egyptian and Greek and Jewish and Oriental religion and magic intermingled. The Greeks who came to Egypt were very open-minded about the local gods. The experience of Mediterranean paganism made it easy for them to identify Amun with Zeus or to say the Egyptians worshipped Aphrodite the Goddess of Love under the name of Hathor.

How this worked in practice can be seen in the Kom el-Shukafa tomb deep below the streets of Alexandria, which dates from the second century AD. At first sight it looks like a typically Egyptian tomb fronted by papyrus columns with the winged disc of the sun behind, and a row of cobras' heads along the façade. But when we look closer we see figures in ancient Egyptian poses but with Graeco-Roman faces. On either side of the door are guardian serpents, but carrying the snake-entwined staff of Hermes, the Greek guide of souls. Inside the tomb itself the sarcophagi are decorated with traditional Greek funeral motifs: bunches of grapes, wreaths, cattle-skulls and masks, but above them are the ancient gods of Egypt. Isis is protecting the sacred bull with her outstretched wings; Thoth the God of Wisdom is there; the hawk-headed Horus tends the mummy of the dead. There is even the jackal-headed Anubis, the guardian of the dead, wearing Graeco-Roman military gear. This then is the strange synthesis that emerged in Hellenistic and Roman Alexandria, the 'crossroads of the entire world' (Dio of Prusa, *c*.70 AD).

FROM THE ANCIENT WORLD TO ISLAM

We now come to one of the most difficult of historical questions: not simply why do civilizations decline and fall, but what is it that causes a complete shift in their way of seeing? How are we to account for a change as apparently cataclysmic as that from Pharaonic Egypt to Islam? It is perhaps the key question of Egyptian history. In the last century BC and the first AD, in the great cultural zone of the Hellenistic world, which extended as far as India, there was a tremendous stirring-up of religious ideas which would eventually undermine all the old orders in those lands, the heartland of civilization. The revolutionary ideals of the Axis Age now came home to roost. The old gods were fading away, in the Nile Valley, in the Fertile Crescent, in Iraq and in Arabia. New spiritual movements rose up everywhere, mono-theistic, polytheistic, mystical, transcendent. New gods appeared, and strange sects: sacrificial, ecstatic, and mystery cults. The old sacred languages in their cumbersome scripts (cuneiform, hieroglyphic) are replaced by the flexible demotic *linguae francae* of Greek and Aramaic. Great cosmopolitan cities such as Alexandria and Antioch became centres of religious speculation and of mass cults for the urban poor. In Alexandria there was even a Buddhist community, and sects of 'Gymnosophist' drop-outs who lived semi-naked, bathing in the Nile and practising asceticism like Hindu Brahmins. On the one hand there was a rise in irrationalism and mystery cults, and on the other a search for 'gnosis', interior knowledge, as opposed to ritual-based religion. In recent years Gnosticism has come to be seen as a universal religious phenomenon which virtually constitutes another world religion.

We can trace the spread of these ideas of a personal path to salvation through the Qumran community's Dead Sea Scrolls, through early Christianity, to the Mandaeans of Iraq and the Manichaeans, whose Iranian brand of Gnosticism arose in the third century AD. But Egypt was the hotbed of religious syncretism. It is as if the breakdown of their old religious system under the impact of Hellenistic culture and spirituality was so traumatic as to throw up dozens of different sects expressing all these various strands of Near Eastern thought. The remarkable 'Gnostic Gospels' found at Nag Hammadi near Abydos for example represent an entire alternative reading to early Christianity, with quite different ideas about the nature of God, the role of women in the church, and what would become a fundamental point of issue in the early church, the question of damnation and eternal punishment.

From the existence of this bewildering mix of faiths between the first century BC and the third AD we can draw certain obvious conclusions. The old Bronze Age polity was finally breaking down. As Carl Jung wrote of the antecedents of the Hitler era (when even before the First World War he saw symptoms of 'mental change') there was a sense that the old 'metaphysical authority set above this world', was disappearing: 'the first smell of burning was in the air.' One of the most dramatic indicators of this psycho-logical strife was the withering away of the confident outlook of traditional Egyptian civilization. And in particular, as Christianity gained more and more converts among the alienated urban masses in Alexandria and the towns of the Nile Valley, there arose a wholly new feeling in Egyptian culture, nothing less than a rejection of the material world: monasticism. In late Roman Egypt, an upheaval began as momentous as any political revolution. A change occurred in the psyche of Near Eastern culture which has helped shape the Western mind ever since: all along the Nile valley, tens of thousands of people took up the monastic life. There are distant echoes of our own time here; of self-sufficient communes dropping out of society, and of the widespread feeling that civilization itself had failed. 'Better cities may arise one day', said the Egyptian philosopher Plotinus. 'Our children, though conceived in a sinful age, may build better than their fathers.' And so the old fabric of pagan culture, the stable cosmos which had sustained Egyptians for so long, was eroded by Christianity, with its appeal not to a great earthly ruler but to a distant high God. 'This was a time,' said Epictetus, 'when we realized how insecure the human condition is.'

THE END OF EGYPTIAN PAGANISM

In the old towns along the Nile valley the ancient paganism survived right through the Christian era. From the Greek conquest indeed, it took nearly a thousand years for it to break down: an amazing testimony to its resilience. Egypt was perhaps three-quarters Christian by the end of the sixth century AD, the eve of the Islamic conquest. But almost up till that time paganism was still on an organized basis with temple worship, nearly two centuries after edicts from Rome banned the old religion.

Akhmim in middle Egypt was, and still is, a famous textile town. Fragments of its cloths from the late Roman period suggest a rich mixed culture with their Greek, Egyptian and Christian themes. When the Greek traveller Herodotus visited Akhmim back in the fifth century BC he had reported that this was the one city in Egypt whose inhabitants favoured Greek customs. And this was still true right up to the end of the Roman Empire and even until the Islamic conquest. The town had a number of pagan temples, including one to the Greek god Perseus. But its most famous temple was to the ancient phallic god, Min, whom the Greeks identified as Pan. Only finally completed by Trajan in 115 AD, it was described as a wonder of the world by medieval Arab travellers. In 1183 Ibn Jubayr thought it 'the most remarkable temple in the world,' and gives a lavish account of its extraordinary decoration, with painted and carved ceilings, forty huge columns with ornate capitals, and dimensions of about 370 by 250 feet. The demolition of this and other temples of Akhmim began during the fourteenth century, though the ruins of a Roman temple founded by Trajan in the second century were still visible in the nineteenth century. Now in a new excavation remains of the Min temple are emerging from deep below the streets 'east of the city and below its walls' just as Ibn Jubayr says. In 1989 two colossal statues of daughters of Rameses II were uncovered, suggesting the temple as it survived into Islamic times was largely from the Eighteenth Dynasty.

In the fifth century AD, Upper Egypt was famous for its

Greek-speaking literary figures like Olympiodorus of Thebes, who travelled as far as Ethiopia and the Black Sea with a faithful parrot who spoke Attic Greek 'and could pronounce his master's name!' In Akhmim was a circle of pagan poets who travelled widely in the Eastern Empire. Among them was Nonnos, who wrote an enormous epic poem in Greek, running to 48 books, as long as the *Iliad* and the *Odyssey* combined, on the subject of Dionysus, the pre-eminent pagan god of late antiquity, the god of frenzy and intoxication. Such figures help us identify the intellectual and psychological changes happening in Egypt before Islam. Out of this world have come the recent Upper Egyptian papyrus finds, of alchemical, magical and astrological texts, of occult and pagan philosophy. In this cultural milieu the alchemist Zosimus of Panopolis had worked, mingling Platonism and Gnosticism with Judaism and 'oriental wisdom'. This too is the world in which Horapollon, a distinguished late fifth-century pagan, could still attempt to write a treatise on the interpretation of hieroglyphic signs. Horapollon's father Asclepiades had produced a literary history of the early traditions of Egypt stretching back over 30,000 years! No wonder then that the temple of Min survived long after the Emperor Theodosius' edict against the pagans.

Most of the well-to-do landowners around Akhmim were still Greek-speaking pagans in the fifth century; in fact there are cases in the neighbourhood of town councillors who went back to paganism having been converted to Christianity. This is the background to the situation that arose in the early fifth century, when the militant Christian abbot, Shenuda of the White Monastery, which still stands over the river from Akhmim, launched night raids with fanatical monks to beat up neighbouring pagan landowners outside the town. Finally the monks attacked the temple of Min itself, stealing a statue of Min and some sacred books. But the standing of the pagan priests in the community was still great enough for them to take Shenuda to court and sue him for his vandalism. Elsewhere in Upper Egypt the culture of Hellenism survived into the sixth century. In Nubia the temples of Philae for example were not closed until the reign of Justinian (527–65) when they were taken over for Christian services. By then their pagan priests were illiterate and impoverished; knowledge of the hieroglyphs long reduced to mere magical mumbo-jumbo. Up till the second century AD towns like Akhmim and Oxyrhynchus had still employed traditional stone-cutters to do monumental glyphs. But that century was the dividing line. Afterwards knowledge of the old writing was reduced to a small élite. The last inscriptions come from the fourth century and are largely gibberish. When Horapollon wrote his treatise on hieroglyphs not long before 500 AD, he no longer knew what they meant. Soon enough, this son of the pagan author of a 'Harmony of all theologies' converted to Christianity. It was a sign of the times.

In the sixth century, all over Egypt the temples were vandalized before conversion into churches. At Abydos, Christian fanatics chiselled away with careful malice at those intimate gestures which had connected ancient men and women with their old gods. At Luxor, a Coptic church was built inside the sanctum of the great temple of Amenophis III; at Medinet Habu the wall carvings were hacked away, obliterating the face of Isis and the phallus of Min. A revolution of the mind was now taking place: a movement from the worship of many gods to that of a single God. Out of this crisis emerged Islam: the final stage of the transformation of the religion of Abraham through the Jews and Christians to the last great world religion proclaimed by the prophet Mohammed, realigning Egypt to her age-old connections to the east across the Red Sea.

ISLAMIC EGYPT

In 641 AD, after a thousand years of Greek and Roman rule, Egypt fell to Muslim Arabs bearing the new faith of the prophet Mohammed. But life in Edfu went on apparently unmarked by these shifts in regime. Until 700 AD the bureaucracy worked in Greek, as it had for centuries. Only gradually did the change become apparent, as the cultural life of Egypt after so long looking towards the Mediterranean turned again to the Fertile Crescent.

In Edfu, as throughout the Mediterranean and Near Eastern worlds, the Christians and the Muslims were the inheritors of the ancients. And the effects of that tremendous revolution at the end of the late antique world still shape our lives today. One of the last Greek religious papyri from late seventh-century Egypt sets the seal on that revolution. For it gives in Greek the words which are central to the creed of every Muslim, 'In the name of God the merciful and the compassionate, there is one God and one God alone,' and it continues, in Greek, *Mahmet Apostolos Theou*, 'Mohammed is the apostle of God.' With that to all intents and purposes the world of Isis, Hathor and Aphrodite had passed.

The change to Islam though would take many centuries. A census from around 700 showed the countryside was still entirely Christian: '10,000 villages with five million souls.' Mass conversions began in the eighth century after a long series of rebellions and harsh repression by the Muslim rulers, revolts largely inspired by excessive taxation rather than by religious or communal strife. But Islam only became the majority religion in the tenth century. Today the Christian Copts, though reviving in numbers, are less than ten per cent of the population.

The pre-Christian pagan culture survives today only in folk custom, though out in the countryside, especially in Upper Egypt, the deeper layers of the past are still visible. In mid-March, for example, on the full moon which heralds the onset of the heat of summer, a great festival takes place which still preserves some unmistakable traces of the popular culture of ancient Egypt.

At this time tens of thousands of people come in from the countryside to descend on the little town of Luxor for their great annual festival. Up here people still celebrate the ancient feast days: the Spring Festival, the rising of the Nile and especially the forty days of mourning for the dead which are still observed, as they were in Pharaonic times. Indeed there are many local festivals still to be seen deep in the countryside which are the descendants of ancient cults to holy men and women, to ancient shrines, to trees, snakes and goddesses, now Islamicized and

Christianized. But this is the biggest. It is a festival for a Muslim saint, Abul Haggag, but it takes place at a mosque inside one of the great pagan temples of ancient Egypt; a mosque whose ancient stonework stands perched amid fourteenth-century BC columns on top of twenty feet of accumulated debris. The Coptic Christians also take part, for they too once had a church inside the temple; indeed the Muslim saint's wife was a Copt, and traditionally Coptic women have always sung the saint's lament.

Abul Haggag died in the eleventh century, at the point when Islam was becoming the dominant religion in Upper Egypt. His tomb inside the mosque has been a place of pilgrimage ever since. On the steps, souvenir sellers offer incense, beads, holy charms, and incantation sheets. On the walls as you go in are palm prints in the blood of women devotees, a custom since the Upper Paleolithic period. As everywhere, orthodoxy may demand one thing, but what the people do is another matter and in the worship of sheikhs and saints, the ordinary people, the fellahin, fill the void between their daily hopes and fears and that distant high God. After the songs and prayers round the tomb the night is passed in passionate celebration with the traditional music and songs of Upper Egypt. The two lands of Upper and Lower Egypt were united by Menes the Hawk King five thousand years ago, yet all those long years of union have not completely concealed the join. Even today they are still two lands, each with its own character, customs and traditions, and a man from Cairo or the Delta would feel a stranger here tonight. Indeed perhaps Haggag's festival is as near as we can get today to the ancient celebrations for the renewal of life each year with the resurrection of Osiris.

Next day the festival reaches its climax. The living descendants of the saint lead a huge procession around the ancient temple and its mosque, bearing representations of the coffins of Haggag and his sons. Behind them comes Luxor's guild of ferrymen with their ceremonial boats. They are carried on trucks these days, but nonetheless the ferrymen are discharging their traditional duty, just as their ancestors did thousands of years ago, when around the streets of ancient Luxor they bore the boat of the Sun-God Amun. The day ends not in solemnity, but in carnival with drinking, dancing and sexual licence: un-Islamic perhaps, but true to the spirit of the ancestors. Indeed it strongly recalls Herodotus' account of the joyful and licentious festival for the goddess Bastet in the fifth century BC. 'When the Egyptians travel to it, they do so like this: men and women sail together and in each boat there are many persons of both sexes. Some of the women make a noise with rattles, and some of the men play pipes for the whole journey, while the others sing and clap their hands. If they pass a town on the way they stop, and some of the women land and shout and mock the women of the place, while others dance and lift up their skirts. They do this at every town along the river, and when they arrive they consume more wine than in the whole of the rest of the year. Locals say as many as 700,000 men and women, besides children, make the annual pilgrimage.' And so it is today.

Meanwhile across the river, in the green fields below the western cliffs, is the land of the dead. The great mortuary temple of Rameses III at Medinet Habu lies still partly encumbered with the mudbrick ruins of the Coptic Christian village which was cleared from its rubble-choked courtyards in the nineteenth century. Outside its gate is a small sacred tank, still full of water. Here childless Christian and Muslim women come in secret to pray for children, at the behest of the female spirit mediums who still exist in popular religion. All this they did in ancient times. As a great modern Greek poet from Egypt, Constantine Cavafy, wrote:

That we've broken their statues,
that we've driven them out of their temples,
doesn't mean at all that the gods are dead.

CAIRO: THE ISLAMIC LEGACY

The ancient legacy also survived in the city. Cairo, 'the mother of cities,' as Ibn Battuta said, 'its numberless buildings peerless in their beauty and splendour. A meeting place of travellers, shelter of the strong and weak whose throngs of people surge like the sea.' Cairo was founded in the tenth century in sight of the ancient capital Memphis and the pyramids of Giza and Saqqara. By then the capital of Menes, 'white-walled Memphis', was a mere fable, 'the city of Pharaoh with seventy gates and walls of iron and copper,' as Ibn al-Fakih wrote at that time; a poor Christian village nestling on its ruins. Soon enough its very name would be forgotten. Over the river, Cairo would become the cultural capital of Arab Islam. Escaping the fury of the Mongol attack of 1258, Cairo and Egypt continued to be the guardian of the rich legacy of classical Arab civilization up to the Ottoman conquest of 1517. The Arab world by then perhaps was no longer the cultural powerhouse of Islam – that honour fell to Persia and to Turkey – but Egypt had become the centre of the Arab world, and so would remain.

And in Cairo even today, in its mosques and universities, we can still find living links with the world of the pharaohs: for medieval Islamic Cairo was a civilization conservative in character, with a strong moral tone, like its ancient predecessor. This was not a culture of the brilliant ecumenical cast of tenth-century Baghdad; nor did it aspire to the mystical synthesis of East and West attempted in Persia. It was rooted, earthy and sensible as it had been in the past: devoted to preserving, elaborating and explaining the legacy, but also, and most importantly, expounding the religious texts, the Koran, the *hadith* (traditions) and the law. In the Al Azhar, the leading teaching mosque of Islam, older than Oxford or the Sorbonne, learning is still the study of the sacred texts, binding the land together as it did in ancient Egypt, still trying to maintain the difficult balance between the secular and the spiritual, between religion and the state in fundamentalist times. Indeed even the physical aspect of medieval Cairo recalls its pharaonic predecessor: with its gigantic royal mosques, its enormous domed Islamic mortuary temples, its cities of the dead, its scribal and religious schools, its myriad neighbourhood prayer halls. The western side of the Nile may no longer be the land of the dead, but this huge-scale sacred architecture is fulfilling the same function as it did of old. (In fact the descendant of the temple lands, the religious waqfs, or endowments, totalling one-twelfth of the cultivated land, were only nationalized by President Nasser in the 1950s.) This then was a civilization which, for all the apparently cataclysmic breaks in its history, not only preserved the essential attributes of civilized life, but also continued to do things in the way its ancestors did. And perhaps these two ideas, inseparably bound up with each other, are a clue to the nature of civilization itself.

IBN KHALDUN ON EGYPTIAN HISTORY

Here in Cairo in the late fourteenth century, those questions of continuity were examined by the greatest of all Islamic historians, Ibn Khaldun. His concerns were the same as ours in this book: the nature of civilization, its rise and decline. He considered that settled co-operative human life was the goal of civilization, that it went in cycles of growth and decay like all forms of life. He thought incidentally that over-consumption in society was an inevitable cause of decline. But he believed that under certain favourable conditions of geography and climate, of the character and customs of the people, and their sense of group identity, culture could acquire a rootedness that he called the 'habit of civilization.' And in all history Egypt was perhaps the best example of that habit. The pharaohs, he points out, had political power for three thousand years. They were followed by the Greeks and the Romans, and then the legacy was taken on by Islam. 'So the habit of civilization was continuous here, nowhere else in the world was it more firmly rooted.' And such an idea perhaps helps explain Egypt's continuing cultural leadership in the Arab world. Untouched by the Mongol attacks of the thirteenth century which destroyed Iraq, Egypt remained the dynamic centre of Islam until her conquest by the Ottomans in the sixteenth century; even today she has a rich and pluralist culture which reminds us of her Hellenistic ancestry. At the beginning lay the early Egyptian state, the first comprehensive attempt in human history to satisfy the needs of men and women to live together in an ordered state with a degree of happiness and material well-being. And so far it has been one of the most successful.

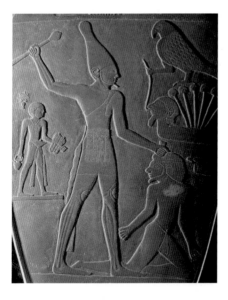

Left: The Narmer Palette (c.3100 BC). The white-crowned king of Upper Egypt kills Wash, a ruler from the Delta, symbolized by a personified papyrus clump on which sits Horus the hawk, Narmer's patron deity.

Below: King Menkaure (Mycerinus) between the goddess Hathor and the personification of Hu nome (province), c.2500 BC. The brilliant artistic tradition of the Old Kingdom survived until the Greek period.

Top: The Theban landscape – pink cliffs bordering the green strip of the valley. Until the modern dams were constructed, this was a uniquely balanced environment which formed the basis of civilization.
Above: Weighing the soul, from the Book of the Dead. Some fundamental Egyptian religious beliefs, such as the idea of a Last Judgement, may have later influenced Christianity and Islam.

Top: Saqqara. The jubilee festival courtyard with its stone 'tent shrines' for provincial gods, with Zoser's Step Pyramid behind.
Above: Coffin portraits from the Faiyum, second century AD. 'Look how you have progressed from being a mere human being on the face of this earth,' wrote the Egyptian Christian Origen. 'Be clear, and understand that there is a capacity in each of you to be transformed.'

Right: The Mayan site of Tikal, still partially covered by forest. This photograph, taken in 1882, gives an idea of what the early archaeologists saw.
Below: 'Now it ripples, now it murmers, empty under the sky' (Popol Vuh). Lake Atitlan, Guatemala, one of the four sacred lakes that still mark the quarters of the world of the Quiche Maya.
Opposite top: Machu Picchu, Peru – a royal residence and mortuary shrine built by Pachacuti Inca in the 1440s, abandoned after the Spanish Conquest in the sixteenth century.
Opposite bottom: The ball court in the central plaza at Copan, Honduras, eighth century AD.

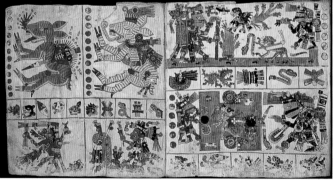

Top: King 'Eighteen Rabbit' of Copan, dated 20 August 731.
Above: Pages from an Aztec codex showing the god Quetzalcoatl. Mexican written traditions of the Spanish Conquest are an important part of our picture of the fall of the New World.

Above: The ancient Mayan festival on the day 'Eight Monkey',
Momostenango, Guatemala. Even in the twenty-first century the
daykeepers burn incense and perform rituals around the 'city of shrines'.
As Las Casas wrote in 1542, 'Everything that has happened since the
marvellous discovery of the Americas has been so extraordinary that it
remains incredible to anyone who didn't see it with his own eyes.'

Above: The Western tradition – the Christian creator-god, standing outside his creation and imparting its laws. This conception of monotheism is as particular to Europe as Shiva's dance is to India.

FIVE

CENTRAL AMERICA
THE BURDEN OF TIME

A HUNDRED AND SIXTY YEARS AGO deep in the jungles of Central America, European explorers came upon the ruins of a vanished civilization. 'In the solemn stillness of the forest,' wrote John Stephens in 1839, 'the monuments were like sacred things, like divinities mourning over a fallen people.' It soon became apparent that the builders of the hitherto unknown cities of Mexico, Guatemala and Honduras, the Maya, had achieved astonishing feats of astronomy, science and mathematics; they had even invented writing independently of the Old World. Sites such as Copan, said its discoverer, were 'like a newly found history, proving that the ancient peoples of the Americas had not been savages, but had equalled the finest monuments of the ancient Egyptians, with skills in art, architecture and sculpture which had not derived from the Old World, but originating and growing up here without models or masters, having a distinct separate and independent existence like the plants and fruits of the soil indigenous.'

These sentiments echoed those of the first Europeans to enter the Americas, at a time when the city civilizations of the Aztecs and the Incas were in full flower. The first conquistadors literally could not believe their eyes: 'We were wonderstruck,' said Bernal Diaz. 'We said that what lay before us was like the enchantments told in the ancient myths. Some of our soldiers even said that what we were seeing was a thing of dreams. Gazing on such wonderful sights we did not know what to say.' The sense of shock experienced by the conquistadors could perhaps only be reproduced today by meeting people of another planet.

The civilizations of America had grown and flowered with no contact whatever with those of the Old World, the Near East, India and China. Yet here were sophisticated societies with great architecture. They had elaborate rituals, writing, science and mathematics and pyramids like those in Egypt. It seemed scarcely credible to Europeans that these native peoples could have created complex societies in many ways rivalling Europe. 'These Indians have high moral virtue,' admitted one sixteenth-century friar. 'Skilled in all mechanical and liberal arts; perfect philosophers and astrologers. In matters of policy they are several steps ahead of those who pretend to greatness in the political arena: and yet,' he went on, 'their religion is an abominable caricature of the message of Christ, and can only be the work of the Devil himself.' It was a great conundrum. The civilizations of the Old World, even the most original, India and China, had all learned from each other as to some degree their histories intertwined. But here was a civilization totally self-contained, which had pursued its own extraordinary vision of human destiny with a stern and amazing constancy. If the physical parallels with the Old World were immediately apparent, the moral differences were profoundly disturbing.

So much about the pre-Columbian Americans seemed totally original to the Europeans, and yet there were also intriguing clues from a deeper common past of all humanity, some of which struck even the earliest scholarly observers, the Jesuits. If we compare the Maya for example with the ancient Chinese, the similarities of belief and practice and symbol suggest that the peoples of the Americas never quite lost the deep connection with their prehistoric origins in Asia. Even today in the Guatemalan countryside you will see the belief in jade, just as in China, for health and death rites. Other parallels are the symbolism of tortoise and bat; divination; the burning of prayers; representations of the tree of life; in some ways the art of the classical Maya and the Chinese is remarkably similar. All of these elements must go back even before language itself, back to some

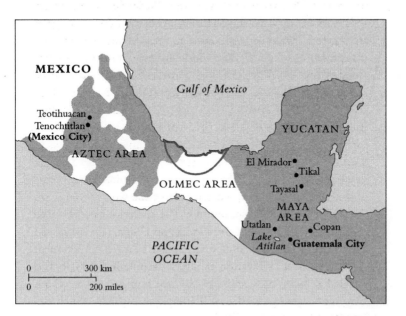

Central America, with the main sites mentioned in the text. The Mexican plain, the Yucatan and the Guatemalan highlands have formed distinctive cultural zones throughout history.

common root of Asiatic humanity which evolved during the long development of Palaeolithic culture in its Chinese heartland. The Maya also shared with the Chinese the fundamental belief that civilization and humankind are not set apart from nature but are part of a natural order whose workings it is the human duty and the human interest to understand And like the Chinese, the Maya did this through divination, shamanism and through intellectual and moral control. At the core of the Mayan view of civilization was an all-consuming obsession with time, time measured in vast recurring cycles of hundreds of millions of years, longer indeed than the universe is known to have existed. Where the Greeks explored the cosmos through geometry, and the Hindus through metaphysics, the Maya explored it through the mathematics of eternity.

Since the landing of Columbus in 1492, two conceptions of civilization have fought for the soul of the peoples of the Americas: the one, foreign and recent, that of the West; the other ancient and native. The struggle between these different visions, the central theme of the last five hundred years of human history, was here fought out with particular violence and intolerance. But despite genocide and forcible conversion, the spiritual conquest of the native Americans has never taken place. For all this time they have tenaciously held on to their old languages, their old beliefs, their old views of the cosmos and of time, keeping faith as they would put it with their 'ancient future.' This chapter then is the story of the destruction of a civilization, and the tenacious survival of some of its ideals in folk culture right down to our own time.

THE SURVIVAL OF THE HIGHLAND MAYA

Our search begins in Chichicastenango, Guatemala. 'Chichi' is one of the market towns in the highlands of the Quiche Maya. Chichi itself was a Mayan settlement before the Spanish Conquest; its two main pre-Conquest shrines still function today. Both are now Catholic churches. The smaller of the two, El Calvario, is strictly out of bounds to Europeans. The larger, St

Thomas, stands over the market stalls, a big flight of steps leading up to the doors. On the steps a traditional fire-altar burns, and travellers burn copal incense in home-made censers, asking forgiveness from the Mayan spirit guardians at the door. All around the market you can pick out the home regions of the traders by their woven jackets. For example Xibalba, the bat, which is an ancient symbol from the Mayan underworld, worn by the last dynasty of the Cakchiquel Maya who ruled here in the Highlands, is today the emblem of the township of Solola, near Lake Atitlan. The designs on the women's blouses, the *huipils,* are the most elaborate, carrying coded information about clan and lineage. It is one of the ways the people have preserved part of the pattern of the old Mayan universe.

In Chichi the traditional civic rituals are kept up by the religious guilds, the *cofradias.* They hark back to pre-Columbian times, organizing the festival days here, both Christian and Mayan. In fact it was through the *cofradias* in Chichi in 1702, that Europeans were allowed to see and copy the only known manuscript of the Mayan genesis, the *Popol Vuh.* Our present knowledge of this great work, which has been translated into many languages, derives from this one version; though Mayan shamans still know its stories, and other manuscripts may well exist hidden from European eyes.

Down the middle of their church are Mayan altars where candles and copal are burned for the ancestors, the shamans and the midwives. At one end of the great barn-like nave, roped to the supports of the balcony, is a huge cross. This is no ordinary cross: it is the magic 'speaking cross' of Mayan mythology, in whose name one of the greatest revolts against the European settlers took place in the nineteenth century. The prayers of the *cofradias* might stand as a text for all the native peoples of the Americas. They also articulate a key theme of our story: the survival of strands of an older culture alongside and even intermingled with its supplanter. 'These rituals of worship,' they say, 'were handed down from our first ancestors, from the time of the first gods, and were never lost,' despite the Spanish conquest.

'Don't expect us to give up these customs, Father Christ, for us only names and fortunes change.'

The discovery of the lost manuscript of the *Popol Vuh* in Chichi illuminates another fascinating aspect of the survival of Mayan culture: the perseverance of *written* testimony. Five hundred years have elapsed since the Europeans first made contact with the civilizations of the New World, five hundred years which saw their conquest, enslavement and the dissolution of much of their culture. In the sixteenth century the Catholic church made a concerted attempt to root out Mayan literature and destroyed the books in formal burnings. Only half a dozen Mayan codices are known to survive today in Western libraries. But you only have to come out to the villages of Highland Guatemala to see that the ordinary people, the descendants of the Maya, have hung on with an almost incredible tenacity not only to some of their most basic beliefs and traditions, but also to the written evidence of their entitlement to their ancestral lands. (Even though today they may still be reluctant to let Europeans see them.) In a little village outside the town of Totonicapan one of the local families bears the name of the last Mayan lord in these parts. Today they are peasant farmers, who live in a big communal room with a stamped earth floor. On one wall, in an elaborate glass-fronted shrine, is the family deity, St James, who has taken on the attributes of the Mayan war god. Incredible as it may seem, the family still possesses sixteenth-century manuscripts including a great book which sets out their legal title to their hereditary lands which they possessed before the Spanish conquest. They have been understandably secretive about the existence of their manuscript. Who can blame them given what has happened to the Maya, in particular the systematic destruction of Mayan literature which took place at the hands of the Catholic church? At the beginning of their family book is a strange map. It shows the sacred central area of the last capital of the Quiche Maya where their early sixteenth-century ancestor was a leading court official. Here are the four main pyramids, the great sacred plaza, the circular altar for the earth god, the ball court and the royal palaces. And underneath is a note by the author writing in the mid-1550s in Quiche which says, 'These are the constructions in stone and in song of the great Quiche.' Remarkably, the compilation of this manuscript took place in the same year or two as the *Popol Vuh* was committed to writing, and some of the leading local Mayan figures from that time are mentioned in the codicils to both books. Clearly in the aftermath of the violent conquest of the Highland Maya, as European domination began to look increasingly permanent, there were those among the Mayan aristocracy who saw the need to look to the future.

The citadel depicted in the book of Totonicapan was destroyed by the conquistador Pedro de Alvarado in 1524. But still the ruins of Utatlan are visited by Mayan shamans, priests or diviners who perform their rituals there on the festival days of their calendar. Theirs is a spirit world maintained in secret for five centuries. The ruins lie surrounded by forests and ravines deep in the Mayan highlands. This is the heartland of the Quiche, an area of resistance to European rule even now. But Utatlan hides an even more extraordinary secret. Right under the citadel destroyed by the conquistadors is a cave running three hundred feet underground. Ever since the fall of the city, ceremonies have taken place here hidden from European eyes. Here the priests pray to the earth, to the ancestors and to the ancient Kings of the Maya, '*Santo mundo*,' '*Dios mundo*,' and '*Rey Quiche*' (Tecun Uman, killed by the Spaniards in 1524). They salute the 'City of holy ruins' itself, and their ancient race, '*Nuestra raza Maya-Quiché*'. They burn tallow candles, sugar and copal, pouring alcohol so that the flames and smoke roar up in the darkness. And from the strange mixture of Christian and Mayan incantations come words to the holy earth from the pre-conquest creation book, the *Popol Vuh*. 'Holy earth, heart of earth, giver of life, give us children, keep them on your green road and let there be continuity within.' Afterwards they light a fire at the mouth of the cave to offer 'a humble thanks to Heaven-Earth,' and the smoke drifts slowly up the cliff face, catching the rays of sunlight, through a tangle of creepers, ferns and wild lavatera. The Maya took many things from the worship of Christ but what it could not give them was the continuing sanctity of Mother Earth.

A final example of the perseverance of Mayan custom comes from deeper still into the Quiche Maya heartland, at Momostenango. In the hills above the town is the house of a Mayan shaman, Andres Xiloj. Andres is a living link with the pre-Spanish world. A priest for fifty years, he is a *Chuchkahau*, a lineage head, literally a 'mother-father.' He is also a daykeeper, a guardian of the Mayan calendar which, astonishingly, is still preserved here. An expert in the traditional ritual of incantation and its sacred language, 'Don' Andres can interpret ancient texts such as the *Popol Vuh*. He became a daykeeper after a severe illness, which decided him to 'give service to the earth.' Part psychologist, part spirit medium, Andres uses sacred divination as a tool to probe the ills of his patients, to 'feel' their past and future, reading the messages given by sensations in his own body. His job ultimately, is 'to bring what is dark into light.' For his patients he lays out the shiny dark red coral tree seeds and crystals according to the days of the Mayan calendar, a 260-day cycle based, so the Quiche believe, on the gestation period of the human baby within the womb. In the Mayan year there are thirteen numbers and twenty signs – for example the day may be six snake, or eight monkey. Some are auspicious, some not. Like many of the Quiche, Andres carries this calendar in his head and can translate into the western calendar in seconds. The preservation of a culture's own time is perhaps a symbol of its will to survive. And for Don Andres, one idea more than any other signifies the difference between the two cultures: for the Maya, the earth is a sacred thing. This was why, in the *Popol Vuh*, humankind was 'given memory to count the days,' to be 'bearers of respect for its divinity; to keep the rituals which connect humanity, nature and the heavens.' Without them the universe would cease to bear meaning, for as Andres says, 'If we make an enemy of the earth, we make an enemy of our own body.'

The story of the Central American civilizations, then, is very different from those of the Old World. Here we are dealing with the violent, deliberate and systematic destruction of a culture in comparatively recent times. Andres' divination, the *cofradias* at Chichi, the Mayan Catholic churches, the lost manuscripts, the rituals at Utatlan: all represent fragments of a collective act of survival, an attempt to keep a universe together five hundred years on from the Conquest. It is the story of how one civilization was conquered and suppressed by another, but refused to accept its values.

THE ARCHAEOLOGY OF ORIGINS

It may be helpful to recall the background here: humans probably entered the Americas from Siberia across the Bering Strait during the last glacial period, between 40,000 and 12,000 years ago, though some archaeologists would bring the earlier limit down to 20,000 years ago. Rising sea levels then isolated the American continent, which developed on its own until 1492, though as we have seen, there are many parallels between the civilizations of the Old and the New worlds: in agriculture, cities, metallurgy, divination, writing and even in symbols. By 9000 BC settlers had reached the tip of South America. By 7000 BC they were cultivating staple crops, especially maize. Agricultural villages have been traced in Central and South America, and in the Andes, by 3000 BC, including large and as yet little-known settlements in Amazonia. The cultural traits of these regions were very long lasting. From the second millennium BC, the Olmecs in Central America and the Chavin in Peru would exercise a pervasive influence on iconography, religion and architecture in their respective spheres right up to, and even after, the European conquest. From them the main American civilizations took their inspiration: Teotihuacan, and the Maya, Toltec and Aztec in Central America; the Moche, Nazca, Chimu and Inca in the Andes. In the extraordinary inner power of the Olmec art of 3,000 years ago, for example, we already feel the grave, stoical sensibility of the Central American universe.

TEOTIHUACAN

The first great flowering of Central American civilization took place in the first millenium AD in the valley of Mexico, and its centre was Teotihuacan, 'the place where men became Gods.' Here the early Mexicans built a vast city, the centre of a trading empire which extended all over Central America. In AD 500 Teotihuacan may have been among the largest cities in the world, with a population of 200,000 people, a vast metropolis laid out on a grid plan with 8 square miles of temples, palaces, and houses. Here, independently of the Old World, they built huge pyramids rivalling those of Egypt and Babylonia, a testimony that although separated so widely by time and space, the human mind still creates the same symbols, the same dreams of bridging the gulf between earth and heaven. An extraordinary discovery made recently under the heart of the Pyramid of the Sun has confirmed that an elaborate cosmic symbolism underlies the layout of the city. It was built over a natural cave; a narrow passage through the lava leading to a seven-pronged chamber dead under the centre of the pyramid. This was the original pilgrimage place which had dictated the siting of the pyramid above. It was the place of emergence of the first ancestors, alluded to in the later creation myth of the Maya, the *Popol Vuh*: birthplace of the Sun and the Moon, the place where time itself began. Very likely Teotihuacan became an important pilgrimage centre. Hundreds of temples have been uncovered within the city, with altars throughout the residential quarters, and ceramic workshops mass-producing figures of gods and pottery incense burners.

This was the first true urban civilization in Central America. Unfortunately no written documents give us clues to the rulers who created this great planned metropolis but if we compare its origins with those of the first cities in Shang Dynasty China, then a common picture begins to emerge of the origin of Eastern city civilization, of what has been called the 'Chinese-Maya continuum'. At the heart of this is the idea of the city as an

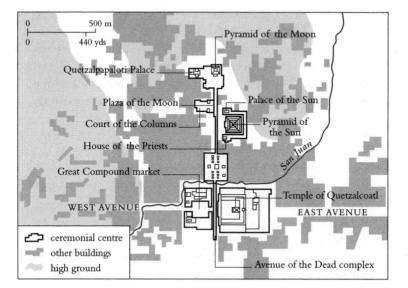

Teotihuacan, the great metropolis of the Mexican plain, c.500 AD. Its ceremonial axes were aligned to the mountains which encircle it and to the constellations. Compare with Madurai (page 77) or Xian (page 99).

earthly pattern of the cosmic order, 'the pivot of the four quarters of the universe,' as the Chinese put it. The same conception is contained in the Inca name for their empire, Tawantinsuga, the 'land of the four quarters' and as we have seen, it may also be valid for the beginnings of Indian, Egyptian and Mesopotamian cities too. At Teotihuacan this idea is immediately striking, with great ceremonial axes intersecting in the four directions, aligned to the surrounding mountains and to the constellations, with the subterranean world represented by the primordial cave under the very centre of the pyramid, whose innermost recesses were illuminated by the sun every summer solstice. Here the city is a ritual theatre where humankind maintains the order of the universe; and in Central America, cities retained that function, even though they might become centres of commerce and trade and so on, right down to the Spanish conquest, when the great Aztec conurbations were still dominated by their ceremonial buildings. Ideology then became one of the driving forces in the development of civilization; religious, social, political, call it what we will. And ideology is also the key to understanding that fateful change which came over humanity with the beginning of civilization, by which – in each of the Bronze Age revolutions which are the subject of this book – the few came to dominate the many, as is still the case across much of the world today.

THE CLASSIC MAYA

During the first millennium AD, urban civilization spread across Central America from the valley of Mexico to the rainforests of Guatemala and Honduras. Until recently it was believed that Teotihuacan was the catalyst for this. But though its influence was felt in trade, perhaps pilgrimage and even in politics, it is now clear that the rise of cities in the Mayan cultural area was an indigenous phenomenon deeply rooted in prehistory. Recent excavations north of Tikal at Mirador have uncovered what must have been the great metropolis of northern Guatemala and southern Mexico which flourished between 100 BC and 150

AD. Discovered in the 1920s but only now mapped and examined, Mirador covered six square miles with tens of thousands of people, its Tigre pyramid the biggest among the Maya, nearly 200 feet high: all of this predating the classic Maya sites such as Tikal. Then from the fifth century AD city states arose right across Yucatan. At the time of the European Dark Ages Tikal, for example, sustained a population of 80,000 with huge irrigation systems and hundreds of dependent villages linked by roads and causeways. At the centre, its vast ritual enclosure had a dozen pyramids and hundreds of altars and shrines; its layout an elaboration of Central American cult practice which goes back two thousand years.

The most intriguing of the Mayan cities is Copan in Honduras. A medium-sized city state of 20,000 people, Copan was ruled by a single talented dynasty from the fifth to the ninth century AD. Its public plazas, pyramids and ball courts – features shared by all Mayan cities – were adorned with wonderful sculpture. Here the Mayan artists demonstrated a prolific imagination and a creative freedom which at times approaches a western naturalism, such as we might find in the best Gothic or Renaissance stone carving (though of course the aesthetic objectives of a Mayan artist were very different). The recent decipherment of Mayan writing enables us to do now what would have been impossible only a few years ago; to enter into the lives, and even perhaps the feelings, of the rulers commemorated here (as yet the lives of the common people elude us). Most extraordinary is a series of portraits of a king we know by his hieroglyph sign as Eighteen Rabbit. These were the images which thrilled the modern world when they were published by Frederick Catherwood in the 1840s. The earliest portrait is the fierce countenance of a man in his prime, his mid-forties, dated 11 October 721. The same king appears on a stele dated 731, ten years on – and is it just our imagination or is this not a softer expression, mellowed with age and experience? Finally late in July 736, there is a crudely executed, almost cartoon-like portrait: strangely sardonic, even perturbed. Two years after this image was dedicated, Eighteen Rabbit was captured by a rival king from the city state of Quirigia and beheaded on 3 May 738, when he would have been in his early sixties. 'It is for kings,' said a Mayan Proverb, 'to eat the bread of sorrow.'

WRITING

Writing was invented in Central America independently, as it had been in the Old World: yet another clue to the common patterns in human development. The greatest monument to Mayan literacy is the hieroglyphic stairway of Copan. Literally a hill of signs, this was a huge stepped ramp 50 feet wide, and 108 feet high, with well over 1,200 glyphs telling the mythic and dynastic chronology of Copan down to 755 AD, when it was dedicated by King Smoke Shell. It is the longest single written inscription in pre-Columbian America, a monument to writing, and to time. A fascinating excavation at Copan which took place through the 1980s revealed more evidence of the function of writing in a late classic Mayan city. At the suburb of Las Sepulturas archaeologists discovered a self-contained compound of forty or fifty buildings grouped around eleven courtyards; among them were houses, temples, shrines, storerooms and kitchens. Dominating the main plaza was a great house in whose reception room was a large stone sitting bench, exquisitely carved with hieroglyphs. Flanking the door were two figures holding conch-shell 'inkpots': scribes. Perhaps then this was the residence of the head of an extended family or lineage group who were the hereditary scribes, ritualists and keepers of the calendar of the kings of Copan around 800 AD. If this is so, it is a distant parallel with the role of diviners and ritualists in ancient Chinese kingship.

The last known king of Copan, Yax Pac, died in the winter of 820. The carving of the last date here was left unfinished on 10 February 822. As historical records go, few offer such a riddling combination of mystery and exactitude! With that the dynasty vanished and the city returned to jungle. A few peasant families continued to farm in the delectable valley of the Copan river for the next three centuries but the land never again supported a city. Around the same time Tikal too was deserted. Soon all the classic Mayan cities had gone. The Mayan collapse is still a great mystery. The land may have become exhausted, the environment destroyed; perhaps the civilization simply lost its nerve. Very likely, as in the parallel cases of the Minoans, Mycenaeans, Romans and even complex modern societies (the former Soviet Union for example) the decline of civilization entailed a combination of many factors: environmental, political, social, climatic, psychological. None of these on its own would have spelt disaster, but in combination they were enough to undermine the functioning and continuance of the social order. As always, the great ritual and government centres were the first to go; far too expensive to maintain when things got tough, they were pointless once the élites had gone. Soon enough the cities were reclaimed by forest, with much reduced peasantry. But the legacy carried on in the hearts and minds of the common people. As we have seen, the cults and customs carried on, still spoken in the Mayan language, and when the Europeans first stumbled on the ruins at Tikal in 1848, the Indians living in the forest could still give their ancient name, Ti'kal, 'the place where the count of days was kept,' where the ancestors had borne the burden of time.

THE AZTECS

With the collapse of the classic Maya, the focus of Central American civilization shifts back to its old heartland, the valley of Mexico. Here ringed by mountains was a wide plain and a great lake, Texcoco, with islands and fertile shores. Today it is all covered by Mexico City. Here in the fourteenth century a warlike tribe settled who called themselves Mexica. The city they founded here, Tenochtitlan, was the precursor of what is today the largest city on earth: then it was a stone-built city of 200,000 people situated on an island linked to the mainland by causeways through a vast area of reclaimed swamps.

The story of the Aztec empire which rose here in the fifteenth century is one of the most dramatic episodes in human history. The Aztecs still hold a fearful fascination for us. In their art we feel a tremendous spirituality, but it is spirituality of a kind unlike anything we recognize from our own civilization. The famous statue of the earth goddess Coatlicue, found in the central plaza, the Zocalo, in 1790, was hastily reburied, for fear it might be seen by the youth of Mexico, for fear that they might be exposed to its still dark and potent magic. Dug up and reburied once more in the early years of the nineteenth century, its awe-inspiring presence was still felt to be unbearable. Later still she found a place behind a screen in the University. Today Coatlicue holds a central position in the Aztec room of the National Museum of Mexico City. Her changing fortunes, as Octavio Paz has remarked – from goddess to demon, and from monster to masterpiece – show the changes in our sensibility over four hundred years. Only in our time can we look her in the face, though still not without a sense of unease.

The recovery of Coatlicue, 'the goddess of the serpent skirt,' mirrors our recovery of Aztec history: the story of a growing desire to engage with its 'otherness' rather than simply dismiss it as 'the work of the devil'. The present centre of Mexico City around the Cathedral was also the ritual centre of the Aztec city. Excavation here since the 1970s has uncovered the foundations of the Great Pyramid of the Aztec war god, Huitzilopochtli. This is where the Spanish under Cortés, when they sacked the city in 1521, saw horrific scenes of human sacrifice. Here, said Bernal Diaz, on the night the city fell, his captured comrades were dragged up the steps by the Aztec priests in a last desperate sacrifice to the god of war, on what the Spaniards from then on called the *noche triste*, night of tears. It is one of the most famous passages in the history of the New World: 'Then from the pyramid sounded the dismal drum of Huitzilopochtli, and many other horns and shells and things like trumpets, and the sound was terrifying and we all looked toward the lofty pyramid and saw our comrades being dragged up the steps to be sacrificed. We saw them place plumes on their heads and force them to dance ... and after they had danced they placed them on their backs on narrow stones and with knives they sawed open their chests and drew out their beating hearts and offered them to their idols.'

Blood sacrifice had long been a part of Central American civilization, as it has been part of most cultures. But human sacrifice – ritual killing, as opposed to the shedding of blood – was apparently on a limited scale among the Maya till late on in their history. The Aztecs however believed that the Gods needed blood and the hearts of human victims to nourish them in the struggle with the forces of darkness. Without them, they thought the sun would cease to rise. As they imposed their empire by force and terror over the other people of the Mexican plain, this ideology became more and more extreme, till by the time of the Spanish Conquest thousands could die in a single ceremony. All round the site of the great Aztec temple, the Templo Mayor, archaeologists found grim evidence of their devotions. Ritual deposits from the successive rebuildings of the temple platform included skulls; still in place were the *chacmools* which received the human hearts; there too were the idols which confronted the victims on the steps of the 'artificial mountain,' stone representations of the skull racks on which the victims' heads were mounted, and the obsidian knives with which their hearts were extracted.

Surrounded by the gaiety of Mexico City's street life, the Templo Mayor is still one of those places on earth whose terrible associations seem to linger. How was it that a civilization of such brilliance in the arts, in sculpture, in textiles, in poetry could have been so committed to mass blood-letting and human sacrifice? So that in a four-day festival, as the Spanish relate, ten thousand people could be dragged up the steps of the great temple here to have their hearts ripped out, till the place was 'swimming in blood and reeking to the heavens'. The same questions, it has to be said, have been asked of events in Europe in our own time. When the Spanish saw scenes like this they thought that it must be literally the work of the devil, it was so wholly alien. And yet the Aztecs were only unique in the scale of their killing. Every human civilization has used sacrifice, especially in religion. The theologian and the executioner have been intimates throughout history.

The problem of the Aztecs then is a problem for all of us. And it is a problem which has occupied historians and anthropologists for generations. Why are violence and the sacred so intertwined? Why is death seen as necessary to renew life? Why is killing so ingrained in the psyche of *homo sapiens*? Was *homo sapiens*, who triumphed across the world over all the earlier hominids, also peculiarly *homo necans*, 'killer man'? As yet we can only speculate. The idea that the shedding of blood is necessary for the continuance of life perhaps became deeply rooted in our psyche during the several thousand generations we spent as hunter-gatherers in prehistory: so deeply rooted that bloodshed is still the most powerful symbol of sacrifice even in Western culture today. And the impulse contained in such a symbol can still erupt with atavistic power and violence. The scenes of frenzied killing which Cortés and his followers saw here, with their captured friends being dragged up the steps to their death, were in a sense proof of the Aztecs' piety, (as some of the early Spanish churchmen such as the Dominican Las Casas saw). For uniquely among the great civilizations of the world, they raised solidarity with the universe above *everything*, including human life. In this they could hardly be more different from the humanistic values of the great Old World civilizations, who learned through history, and often from each other, the moderating power of reason; the value of human life, and the need to contain violence in human society by other means (by law, by 'goodness', by religious sanction). To us the Aztec universe may appear irrational, terrifying, murderous in its brutality; and yet it is a mirror held up to our humanity which we ignore at our cost. For in the name of other ideals and other gods Western culture has been no less addicted to killing, even in our own century.

THE FALL OF TENOCHTITLAN

We need not concern ourselves here with a narrative of the events of the Spanish conquest of Central America. Let us simply record a story which may be taken to symbolize the conquest of one vision of time and history by another. By a 52 to 1 chance, Cortés had arrived in the Aztec year 'one reed', when their ancient prophecies said the God Quetzalcoatl would return from exile in the east. For the Aztecs, whose confidence in the recurring cycles of history, the burden of time, was no less than that of the Maya, the coincidence drained away their will to resist. If the Spanish historians of the time are to be believed, the Aztecs immediately understood that these mysterious outside powers would be fatal to their own universe.

On the terrible final night when Tenochtitlan fell, an omen appeared to the Aztecs which for them symbolized the break-up of their mythic and cosmological order. The story is told by Fray Bernardino de Sahagan in his great *General History of the Things of New Spain*, and it came from Mexican informants. 'At nightfall it began to rain but more like a heavy dew than rain. Then suddenly the omen appeared, burning like fire in the sky. It wheeled in huge spirals like a whirlwind giving off light in showers of sparks like red hot embers. It made loud noises rumbling and hissing like metal on a fire. It circled above the walls near the lake shore. It hovered for a while above Coyoncazco (at the shore end of the great western causeway). Then it moved out into the middle of the lake where it suddenly vanished. No one cried out when the omen came into view. The people knew what it meant and they watched in silence.'

GUADALUPE: THE OLD GODS LIVE ON

After the conquest, the Spanish set about systematically to dismantle Aztec culture. But today the brilliant culture of Mexico, so prolific in literature and the visual arts, is still in a real sense a synthesis of native and European belief and sensibility.

163

That native pre-Columbian vision still lives on in the Mexican soul, since independence in 1821, nurtured in a democratic atmosphere, as opposed to the tyranny endured till today by the Maya. We can see the continuities still in the greatest pilgrimage in the Americas: the Virgin of Guadalupe outside Mexico City, which attracts two million devotees on her feast day in December, is a conflation of Christian and pre-Columbian practice and traditions. Her shrine stands on the site of that of an Aztec mother goddess, Tonantzin, and today's worshippers still address the Virgin Mary by that name.

Strange as it may seem, the Christian mysteries formed a bridge between the new and the old faith. Perhaps the reason is not hard to find. The central image of Christianity is the sacrifice of Christ himself: the god who gave his blood and body, even his sacred heart, to save the world. (From sixteenth-century Jesuit art to Freda Kahlo and the surrealists, the severed heart is a potent and continuing theme in Mexican art.) In Christianity, the Aztecs could see the key conception of their religion elevated onto a mystical plane: united in the cross, the ancient Meso-American symbol of the Tree of Life, 'the green tree of the whole world'.

The same pattern can be observed in the Inca civilization in South America. There the sacred topography still endures; the shamanistic cult of the ancestors, which was so important to the Inca state, survives throughout the Andes. And just as in Mexico and Guatemala, the old deities still receive their traditional offerings. This is especially true of the cult of sacred mountains resembling that still seen in China. The yearly pilgrimage to the glacier below Ahsangate, east of Cuzco, attracts thousands to the 'Qoyllur Rit', the 'star snow' festival which is named from the rising of the Pleiades and which takes place just before Corpus Christi in the Christian calendar. At this time the 'bear men' or shamans meet, initiate new members, and gather holy water from sacred places on the glacier: a living link with the Palaeolithic shamanism of Central Asia and its mountain worship. Down in Cuzco itself, the old Inca capital, modern doctors and health workers are far outnumbered by the *curanderos*, the traditional healers who intercede with the mountain deities and perform incantations among the peaks. As throughout the Americas, the high culture of the past has been reduced to 'folk culture' by war and conquest, violence, disease and persecution. But it is still alive.

THE NEW ORDER

After the conquest of Guatemala the Spanish built their new capital Antigua in the shadow of the ancient sacred volcanoes, Agua and Fuego. It was intended as a showcase of the ideals of European civilization. But the reality behind this humanistic façade has been called the greatest genocide in history. It is estimated today that at least three-quarters of the native population of the Americas died of disease or violence in the first century of the Conquest, perhaps as many as 50 million people. Among the Europeans who were horrified by what they saw was Jose de Acosta, whose censored report on the evils done to the native Indians has only recently been published. 'The Spaniards must bear absolute responsibility for what is happening here,' he wrote. 'We have betrayed in our deeds what we professed in our words; everyone agrees the most depraved Indians are those who have come into contact with European culture. We have exploited and plundered these poor people to such an extent that it seems the Europeans are more anxious to decide who has the right to plunder them, rather than make any attempt to protect their human rights. We have not given them Christianity and sincerity but under compulsion, fraud and violence. Never has such cruelty been seen in history in any invasion – by Greeks or barbarians.'

LAS CASAS: WHAT IS CIVILIZATION?

In the early days of the Conquest, the Papacy itself urged on the enslavement of the natives in the name of Christ. But it was among the Catholic clergy that the European conscience grew: indeed today they are often conspicuous among the protectors of the natives against their oppressors. The greatest of these early liberation theologians was Bartolomeo de Las Casas, bishop in Coban. A passionate defender of Indian rights, Las Casas' idealism earned him hatred, and the official tide 'Protector of the Indians.' His memory is still revered in the region called in his memory Vera Paz 'True Peace.' Coban is one of the few churches in Guatemala where even today the services are sung not in Spanish, but in Maya. Las Casas would take his case to the King and Queen of Spain themselves, urging on them justice for the Indians. (And gradually he came to realize that his arguments against the enslavement of the Indians applied with equal force to the black slaves from Africa and all the oppressed peoples of the world).

There is an extraordinary sequel to the story of Las Casas, an incident which lights up the history of the sixteenth century like a flash of lightning and continues to illuminate us even today. In 1550 in Valladolid in Spain there took place a public debate between Las Casas and the leading Aristotelian philosopher, Sepulveda. (The two did not actually meet, but each submitted his evidence separately to a royal commission; all this rich body of material still survives.) The questions at stake go right to the heart of the world's problems even today: in essence, what right does the First World have to dominate, enslave or exploit the Third World?

'Are not these people,' asked Las Casas, 'rational feeling human beings with a soul just like the rest of us, and hence entitled to equality of treatment?' Las Casas went on to bring fascinating arguments from his study of Greek and Roman civilization to show that the city states of Central America conformed in most respects to the Greek view of what an ideal state should be: rational, political entities entitled to respect, patience, persuasion and kindness. No doubt Las Casas won the moral debate but as the whole of subsequent history shows, the rulers of the West, the people with power and money, continue to view the indigenous peoples of the world, from the Indians of Central America to the blacks of Africa, as what the Greeks to their discredit termed 'natural slaves'. Europe's progress to civilization, as Las Casas pointed out, has been as long and painful as any.

THE FALL OF TAYASAL

It was a hundred and fifty years after the Conquest that the last independent kingdom in Central America fell. In the remote jungles of northern Guatemala stood the island fortress of Flores, in native speech Tayasal. Here the late Mayan population was a mixture of Mayan and Mexican, which we call Yucatec. The prophetic books of the Yucatan Maya foretold that catastrophe would revisit them every cycle of thirteen *katuns*, 256 or 257 years. The next cycle was due to begin in 1697. Armed with that knowledge the Spanish force attacked on 13 March of that year. In the middle of Lake Peten they overcame the Mayan war canoes, obsidian-tipped arrows useless against Spanish armour and musket fire. The defenders fled and the Spaniards marched uphill to the top of the island to the great temple of Tayasal. It took them a single day to destroy the twelve temples on the island, to smash their thousands of idols and to conclude in the evening by celebrating a mass on the highest point amid the ruins of the great temple where the church now stands. The last independent kingdom of the Maya had fallen. The locals here seemed to have accepted this almost fatalistically, as an inescapable result of their view of the repeating cycle of time. For three times since the tenth century, the cycle of 256 or 257 years had brought them catastrophe. In Maya eyes this was the true burden of time. And today the old count still continues. The greatest catastrophe of modern Guatemalan history, the US-backed coup which overthrew their democracy in 1954, happened exactly 257 years after the fall of Tayasal.

THE MODERN MAYA

Today the Maya, the majority of the Guatemalan population, still live dominated by a European élite. The guerrilla war of the 1980s left 40,000 dead and a million displaced. It is hoped that now, with a new democracy in place, their history will take a different course. The Mayan strategy for survival has remained stubbornly collective. In their great festivals they celebrate the saints as guardians of the community, not as Christian deities. For them identity still resides in the collective values represented by ancestors and community.

The European élites who have ruled Central America for so long had other views of past and future. One of Guatemala's modern dictators, Estrada Cabrera, expressed his faith in the values of European civilization by constructing concrete Parthenons all over the land, monuments to colonial progress, to the triumph of Greeks over 'barbarians'. In the capital, Guatemala City, as all over Central America, the native culture has been swamped by the consumer values of the great neighbour to the north, Uncle Sam. In the city the Indians are submerged, strangers in their own land, widows of the civil war begging in the shadows. But in the countryside things are different – the old universe still holds together.

In the Mayan calendar the holiest of all days is *Wahxakib Batz*, 'Eight Monkey.' On this morning, seemingly out of nowhere, thousands of ordinary Guatemalan Indians converge on Momostenango, 'the place of shrines', in response to a call from a secret world of the spirit. On this day of the year, the nine ancestral shrines in the hills around the town are renewed and propitiated; and from all over Guatemala the daykeepers gather to initiate new shamans who will carry on bearing the burden of time. In the five hundred years since Columbus, these people have lived outwardly in Western time and Western history and yet all the while they have patiently tended a secret universe. At times it may have seemed that their obstinate faithful care of the burden of time would be their downfall but perhaps after all it has been their salvation. For it was the means by which they preserved identity itself down to what is hoped will be a new age of tolerance and pluralism when native Americans may again live in their own history, in their own time.

SIX

THE BARBARIAN WEST

IN THIS BOOK we have seen that the roots of modern civilization, that is, the forms of society in which most of the people of the planet now live, were primarily Asiatic. We have seen that civilization developed in radically different ways in the Near East, China and India, ways which still shape their respective ways of seeing. The oldest and greatest of these, India and China, are still alive in the lands of their birth, while in the Near East, Islam is the successor to the ancients. Together the peoples of Asia constitute the vast majority of the population of the world today. In this last chapter, which forms a kind of epilogue, it is time to consider the rise of the West, and to look at some of the ways in which it has interacted with, learned from, and borrowed from the older civilizations which preceded it. Our aim is to see whether commonly held ideologies of the West have universal truth, as is claimed; or whether they should be seen more as idiosyncrasies born of the European landscape, climate and history.

We frequently speak of the 'triumph of the West' these days; 'the West' has become a state of mind rather than a place, but in this book we have been taking it to mean the culture of Western Europe and its immediate neighbours, with its colonial offshoots in the Americas and elsewhere. It is Western civilization – European, Christian, capitalist, rationalist – which has become dominant in the world since the Renaissance: the first culture to spread its way of life, values and languages right across the world.

But in comparison with India and China, it is recent. There had been relatively complex societies in Western Europe in the Bronze and Iron Ages, but literate urban civilization came as an exotic flower to Western Europe with the Romans and faded away in some parts when their empire collapsed, to be reintroduced in the Dark Ages by the descendants of the barbarians who settled in its ruins, by the Franks, Goths, Angles and Saxons. So medieval culture in Western Europe was the product of comparatively late folk movements in the fourth and fifth centuries AD. Only after this time were some key ideologies adopted, such as Roman Christianity and Latin culture. That such central beliefs are not indigenous, as they are in India and China for example, may be very significant in the long-term history of the culture. On the other hand, the immigrant tradition would remain a powerful model in Western culture: the 'taking of the land' was rooted in Germanic heroic tales, and the parallel founding myths in the Old Testament enabled the Western European barbarians to see themselves as 'new Israelites', heroic migrants bringing the ultimate truth as defined in their holy book. As we have seen, the very idea of ultimate truth is foreign to the Eastern civilizations.

So Western European culture was by no means as deeply rooted as that of the Near East, China and India, and its social and religious beliefs nowhere near as solid, as some medieval Arab commentators noted. Nor did Western Europe ever have political, cultural or linguistic unity, though there were ancient affinities between the northern European peoples who spoke Germanic dialects, and those around the Mediterranean who spoke Romance. As a result, warfare has been prevalent throughout the history of Western Europe. Only since the 1990s has it moved towards unity after centuries of ferocious inter-state wars which have claimed millions of lives even in our own lifetime. Whether Western history is uniquely violent is difficult to say. All civilizations have been prey to the contradiction between their ideals and the reality of their history; none, after all, has succeeded in containing violence. The West's triumphs on the other hand need no repeating here. Its individualistic conception of freedom was a great gift to the world, and very likely was deeply rooted in its individualistic regional cultures, born in its soil and climate. Its brilliance in art, literature and music is unsurpassed. But in the last five hundred years it is the West which has dealt in death and destruction in every corner of the globe. To try to understand why, let us look at the main strands which make up the tradition.

THE LEGACY OF GREECE

The role of the Greek tradition in European culture is problematic. Should we even view Greece as part of the West? The question may seem perverse, but where a Muslim scholar in tenth-century Baghdad would unquestionably have seen himself as the intellectual heir of classical Hellenism, the idea may never have occurred to a tenth-century scribe in England. She would have been familiar with some of its stories and myths; indebted too to the great patristic legacy in Greek; but she would hardly have thought herself its heir. Israel and Rome loomed far larger in her imagination. The West's invention of Greece as its great spiritual ancestor took place much later, beginning after the eighteenth-century Enlightenment when the role of traditional religion in the West began to fade before modern secularism and science. Then new, and more impressive, intellectual antecedents were needed to corroborate Europe's growing supremacy over older and greater civilizations. Prior to the Enlightenment too, classical Greek culture had been mediated through Roman culture with its rationalistic aesthetic, and through Roman Christianity with its patriarchal authoritarianism. It was the Roman view of Greece which was articulated in the Renaissance and set on a pedestal in the Enlightenment. Only in the mid-eighteenth century did Western Europeans begin to be able to study, for the first time, surviving elements of real Greek culture – landscape, buildings, customs – and especially the people of Greece who, though impoverished and brutalized under centuries of Turkish rule, had clung on to the ancient holistic view of nature which the West and Europe lost with the Enlightenment and the modern scientific view of life: a clue, however indistinct, to the real nature of the classical Greek achievement.

Greece in fact was always the intermediary between Europe and Asia. In the Bronze Age she was first to receive the palace-based civilization of the Near East, but this was not deeply rooted, and when the palaces went, so did the civilization. Similarly in the sixth century BC she was the first to assimilate the new scientific philosophical ideas coming out of Asia, from Iraq, Iran and India, in the Axis Age. In the early fifth century BC these were transformed by the Greek genius into one of the greatest eras in world culture.

The heyday of classical Greek civilization was very brief – the first half of the fifth century BC. The astounding Riace bronzes, the statues from Olympia, Pindar, Aeschylus, the Eleusinian mysteries, the new science of Ionia, the fledgling democracy of Athens and its victories over the Persian empire constitute the familiar landmarks, the fullest realization of a spiritual tradition. The later fifth century, from the Periclean age to Plato, for all its brilliance, was perhaps the overripe coda to one of the most amazing epochs in world history. So familiar indeed are these landmarks that it is easy to miss the uniqueness: neither East nor West perhaps, but a peculiar transformation effected on Greek soil. By 400 BC it had fallen apart in imperialism, in the collapse of democracy, in the horrors of the Peloponnesian War, in political disaster and in a failure of nerve on which Plato would look back with haunting nostalgia. The fifth century Enlightenment opened up every possibility, but it did not lead to a golden age. Greece never united, remaining instead a land of warring city states, and in the mid-fourth century they fell to the brutal and vigorous Macedonians from the north. With that, Athens lost for good its cultural eminence which passed to the great Hellenistic foundations in Asia and North Africa, the powerhouses of a multi-racial empire which spread from the Balkans to India. It was the ideals of this

Hellenistic Age, adapted by the Romans, which would be the first shapers of the Western tradition.

THE GREEK CONQUEST OF ASIA

'The Greeks,' said Aristotle, 'are intelligent and free and have the capacity to rule all mankind.' In the fourth century BC, under Aristotle's pupil, Alexander the Great, they invaded the near East, overrunning Anatolia, Syria, Palestine and then Egypt. The Greek era in Asia, known as the Hellenistic, is now seen as one of the most revolutionary in world history.

Within a generation, the valley of the Nile thronged with Greek colonists, as if on a gold rush. The civilization of Egypt, ancient, mysterious and exotic, made a deep impression on Greek minds. In upper Egypt the monuments were covered with graffiti by awestruck Greek tourists. The native Egyptians, as we can now see from oracular and apocalyptic papyri, were strongly resistant to these new outsiders, as they had been in the past. (This was nothing new: Herodotus had written that 'they keep the ancestral laws and add none other in avoiding foreign customs.') In a prophecy of the Greek period, native Egyptians looked forward to the day when the 'foreign civilization planted among us will fade away; these foreigners who occupy Egypt will disappear like autumn leaves.' Others were more open in their hostility. 'These Greeks are thieves and upstarts, addicted to violence,' fumed one Egyptian priest. 'To think we taught them all they know.' And at Luxor still today, in the inner shrine of the ancient Egyptian temple, striding like a Pharaoh of old, is the violent golden boy of Western history, Alexander himself.

Moving eastwards into Asia, the Greeks conquered the ancient civilization of Babylonia; the old cities of Uruk and Babylon became Greek colonies in a foreign land. It was, said a Babylonian oracle, 'a time of misfortune for our people. But one day it will pass.' Passing the Zagros mountains the Greeks now crossed the Oxus river into Central Asia, founding cities which still flourish today, as far as Samarkand. Through the Khyber Pass they poured into India, building their colonies on the north-west frontier, which formed the basis of a long-lasting Indo-Greek culture in these parts.

In one of the least known episodes in ancient history, Alexander's successors went further still. In the second century BC they sent devastating expeditions down the Ganges, sacking the ancient religious centres of Benares and Patna. In the village of Kausambi modern archaeology has uncovered graphic evidence of the trail of destruction. Here a Buddhist monastery has been excavated which was swept by a Greek firestorm, torched by Greek mercenaries sweltering by the Jumna, so far from home. (Strangely enough, the Hellenistic generalissimo responsible for this, Menander, ended his days as a Buddhist, according to Indian tradition!)

'These were terrible times,' said the Indians. 'The vicious but valiant Greeks ruined our land with fire and famine, killing women and children and even our cows.' Theirs was a revolutionary epoch, an age like our own: restless, cosmopolitan, self-aware, fascinated by sex and violence. And at its heart, just as in the last three centuries, was the brutal appropriation of other cultures. In India they saw the writing on the wall. 'With such strength, implacable will, and cruelty, the heirs of the Greeks will rule the world in a future age.' As Europeans see their history, this was the first time the West went out to the world.

THE BEGINNINGS OF ONE WORLD

But the Greek conquests liberated tremendous historical energies. The dazzling internationalism of the Hellenistic era laid the foundations of a common culture, with common ways of seeing, to much of the land between Egypt and India, which may have played a key role in the formation of the later Islamic world. The Hellenistic age also opened up the economies of the Old World civilizations. Trade routes now opened through Central Asia on the Silk Route to China. 'In earlier times,' said the second century BC historian Polybius, 'the world's history had been a series of unrelated episodes, but from now on history becomes an organic whole. The affairs of Europe and Africa are connected with those of Asia and all events bear a relationship and contribute to a single end.'

In the second century BC the Chinese sent missions into Western Asia, where they became aware of the Parthian Empire in Persia, and heard of the Greeks beyond. This had a tremendous effect on their view of the world. Moving in the other direction, in the first century BC, Greek navigators discovered the secret of the timing of the monsoons. Then Greek and Roman merchants could sail every year across the Indian Ocean to trade in spices, pearls and Chinese silk. Soon the Roman balance of payments ran millions into the red to fill the pepper barns by the River Tiber. Greek colonies could be found as far away as Afghanistan; according to Tamil poems their merchants also resided in South India, organized on lines not unlike the 'factories' of the seventeenth-century India trade. One of the most fascinating books to come down to us from the ancient world is the first-century manual of an Alexandrian merchant describing all the ports of East Africa and India, listing their produce: spices, pearls, silk, ivory. Not surprisingly in the first two centuries AD there were also official embassies between the Romans and the Indian kingdoms: the numerous finds of Roman bullion in Tamil Nadu date from this time. In 166 AD there was even a Roman embassy to China. Archaeological evidence for the staging posts in the East–West trade by sea has now come to light; including a Roman entrepôt near Pondicherry in South India with ware-houses full of Arretine wine, and a remarkable town in the Mekong Delta, Oc-eo, where a large Indian colony dealt in goods from as far away as Persia and the Mediterranean. Through such connections a statue of the Hindu goddess Lakshmi could find its way to a house in Pompeii (79 AD) and a statue of Poseidon could end up in Kolhapur south of Bombay! Such exchanges also took place on land routes. The astonishing storeroom excavated at Begram near Kabul and dating from around 100–300 AD, contained Chinese lacquer work, Egyptian porphyry vessels, Greek glass, and Hindu carvings from the Jumna valley! Soon enough, even temples in Japan would be adorned with treasures from Persia and Byzantium.

So the last centuries BC and the early centuries AD were the beginnings of a vast exchange of cultures and ideas across the Old World. And it is no accident that the great universalist religions arose out of this era – Christianity from the first century, Manichaeism from the third, Islam from the seventh: all had reached China by the late seventh century, travelling along with all the other commerce and exotica, both by the Indian sea route and the Silk Route through Central Asia. The first glimmering of a world economy also appeared at this time, an economy centred in Asia which would begin to take off in the tenth to twelfth centuries, only to be cut short by the Mongol invasions, then to be overtaken by the rising commercial and maritime power of Western Europe.

THE RISE OF ROME

It was not the Greeks but the Romans who laid the foundations of the Western domination of the world. For it was they who first united the Mediterranean world and Western Europe, the core of what we mean by the West still today. Their empire like all empires was built on military might, on slavery and on cruelty. Well organized administrators, brilliant architects, engineers and military planners, the Romans conquered the ancient 'undeveloped' regional cultures of Europe, the Iron Age natives of Gaul and Britain, along with the sophisticated citizens of Greece, Egypt, Syria and North Africa. For the first time, Western Europe was directly brought into the influence of Mediterranean, African and Asiatic civilizations. In places the Romanization was only slight; in Britain for example, after Rome, the cities were abandoned and the élites went back to native traditions of organization. But it was a start.

At its height the Roman Empire extended from Hadrian's Wall in Britain to the Persian Gulf and you could call yourself a citizen of Rome whether you lived in Manchester, Athens, Luxor or even briefly Uruk, in the baking south of Iraq. But unlike India or China, there was no binding religious or social ethic to hold such disparate parts together and in the fourth century it entered a great crisis, economic, social and especially spiritual. It was a time when many different new religious cults and sects were in rivalry, most of them drawing on the old traditions of the Near East and Persia: Judaism, Gnosticism, Zoroastrianism. But out of this spiritual ferment the Christians were in the right place at the right time and, sponsored by the newly converted Emperor Constantine, theirs became the official religion of the Roman Empire in AD 330. From then on, the ideologies of earthly and heavenly empire would be inextricably bound up in Western culture.

The triumph of Christianity is another example of the extraordinary fertility of ideas born in the intractable landscapes of Judaea, Syria, Palestine and Iraq: a testimony to the continuing inspiration which the West has drawn from the more ancient cultures to the East. For the first time in history a religion with universalist ambitions had taken firm root in lands and cultures far from, and unrelated to, those of its birth. A set of beliefs, myths and taboos deriving from the Iron Age people of Palestine and ultimately the Bronze Age cities of Iraq, was accepted by the rulers of Western Europe as the final revelation of history! And even though the Roman Empire itself fell to the northern barbarians in AD 410, this sense of historical mission was never lost. Indeed there is a sense in which Rome has never fallen. For Roman cultural ideals, Roman imperialism and Roman Christianity have remained at the heart of the ideals and the ideologies of the West. And the several renaissances in Western history have been attempts at the rebirth of those ideals. Even the moves to unite Europe that began in the 1990s can be seen in this light: in that sense all Europeans, and most Americans, are heirs to this culture. But unlike China and India, which show an essential continuity of vision throughout their long history, it was only at this comparatively late moment that the West acquired its self, for now the barbarians became the Romans and created a new culture which is the basis of ours even today: the barbarian West.

THE DARK AGES

After the fall of the Roman Empire, tribes of Germanic barbarians made their new home in the ruined provinces. Out on the wild shores of Britain, with a religion from the Near East, a monasticism from Egypt and a written language from Italy, the Anglo-Saxons started to build their new order with the optimism of all immigrants thrown on strange shores.

On the River Tyne in Northumbria, the searcher for that past has to travel back through many histories, through the ruins of later empires built on coal, steel and ships. But at Jarrow is a place as crucial as any in the Western story. Here in the monastery of SS. Peter and Paul, one of the first great histories of the West was written. It spelt out the West's view of its own destiny and was written in Latin by a descendant of the barbarians. The author was a monk here, the Venerable Bede. Bede was the first to popularize the Anno Domini system of dating history from Christ's birth, which is now used throughout the world. The books written here give clues to his world. The biblical hero David, for example, was a model for the rulers of the new dynasties of the barbarian West, portrayed as the psalmist, the teacher of his people. In the same manuscript, David is shown with the spear of God waging just wars against non-believers. Put the two ideas together and you have an image of the ideal Western ruler from the Crusades to the Gulf War of 2003.

Bede's history was the most remarkable and the most successful attempt to show how the peoples of the barbarian West, in the Dark Ages, transformed themselves through the agency of civilization: Christian, Latin, Mediterranean civilization. Bede was a thorough-going European in that respect. In comparison with say contemporary Tang China, Bede's Anglo-Saxons and the people of Europe were indeed barbarians. They were, as we would say today in the patronizing language of the rich, impoverished, underdeveloped, Third World immigrants; and yet here on the Northumbrian coast in the eighth century were already the key elements out of which the culture of the modern West would emerge: Judaeo-Christian religion and ethics, the remains of Greek and Roman humanism and law, native Germanic society and language. In the hands of an historian like Bede, that mixture could be made to tell a powerful story, the story that kings and peoples of the barbarian West were appointed Christian heirs of the Roman Empire, a chosen people destined to lead us on into the last phase of human history from the city of man to the city of God. And that idea, that history is purposive and leads to an appointed end, would become one of the driving themes of world culture from St Augustine to Marx, and from Jarrow to Tiananmen Square.

THE ROOTS OF THE MODERN WEST

In the medieval era between the eleventh and the thirteenth centuries the barbarians came of age. They created one of the greatest epochs of art and architecture which the world has ever seen: the age of cathedrals. But even then, social forces were at work which would eventually loosen the hold of the church of Rome on the former barbarians. In eastern England, eight hundred years ago, changes can be detected in ordinary people's lives which would have a crucial bearing on the future. This is not the history of great events, but the intimate human story of birth, marriage, and childbearing, and it brings us to one of the most fascinating questions in the story of the rise of the West. How was it that such small-scale countries and economies could end up dominating the world as they have done? As late as 1550, England only had two and a half million people. China and India with their vast and highly developed economies had passed 100 million centuries before. They had made all the great inventions necessary for scientific and industrial revolutions. How did the Western European countries overtake them? Was there something distinctive about the character of the West? Or was it just historical chance?

Across north-west Europe, and especially in eastern England, records of birth, marriage and death suggest that as early as the twelfth century a distinctive character was emerging; of late marriage, of small mobile nuclear families, but also of a possessive property-based individualism. Here too are signs of a free market philosophy, which looks uncannily like the seeds of later Western ideology – of the ideology which through the English, French and American revolutions became the dominant philosophy of the West, and which rules our lives even today. In England in particular such ideas may be very deeply rooted. Why is not clear; its insularity may have helped preserve the lineaments of more archaic egalitarian traditions of Iron Age northern peasant farmers. It was also only lightly Romanized. But English common law is certainly Anglo-Saxon in origin; so are the 'democratic' institutions in which it was enacted, the shire and hundred courts. In the tenth century already we can trace the parallel developments of local government, a strong currency and personal freedom, as against slavery. Numerous cases of manumission of slaves for cash indicate that slavery was now being rejected in favour of freedom and money as a more useful basis for society: the nexus of law, currency, personal freedom and representative government with which we are so familiar today may have deep roots in the West.

People were also marrying later, a crucial factor in economic growth and population control. For the younger you marry, the more generations there are in a century. In poor countries, people marry young and have large families: this is the real trigger to overpopulation, and it is at the heart of the world's population problems today. In parts of medieval Western Europe however, men and women were already making 'prudential marriages' – marrying in their late twenties, having small families and practising impartible inheritance. So Western people were beginning to do what today's Chinese, for example, have had to enforce by law.

This was the key not just to population control but to the accumulation of wealth. For with security of life, inheritance, and property, you do not need big families. So the West was already becoming a mobile property-based society, moving away from the extended family and the old continuities of residence and occupation. It is the first sign of a revolution in values which would see the modern West diverge from all traditional societies, the first sign of Western individualism. These individualistic agrarian societies could be found in other parts of northern Europe, especially in Germany and Holland. Theirs was a distinctive way of seeing the world, no doubt, as with India or China, deeply rooted in climate, landscape and soil, the influences which mould the way people organize themselves in history. Theirs was a conception of freedom based on property and common law, the rights of the ordinary man: a conception which derived from Europe, not from ancient Athens. It gave birth to one of the glories of the Western tradition, the idea of an open society. It centred on individual rather than on collective rights and it was a philosophy which, for a time at least, would inherit the earth.

RENAISSANCES IN ISLAM AND THE WEST

Between the eighth and the eleventh centuries the great powerhouse of culture in western Asia was still the Fertile Crescent. The Muslims had inherited the legacy of the ancients and it was in medieval Baghdad that the first attempt was made to bridge the religions and philosophies of East and West. Through the universities and libraries there, Babylonian astronomy, Hindu mathematics and Chinese science were transmitted to Europe by Arab humanists. Here Arab scholars created a brilliant synthesis of Persian, Greek, Jewish and Muslim philosophy and metaphysics; it was one of the great multi-cultural epochs of all time. In tenth century Basra a circle of scholars known as the 'Brethren of Purity' expressed their aims in words which would scarcely be thinkable today. 'If one could combine Arabic faith and Jewish intelligence,' said one, 'with an Iraqi education, Christian conduct, Greek knowledge, Indian mysticism and a Sufi way of life, this would be the perfection of humanity.' That dream still stands as one of the greatest of all declarations of faith in an international civilization.

When Western humanism revived in Italy in the Renaissance it would owe much to the Muslim transmission of the ancient Greek legacy, and to these great waves of civilization which still came out of Asia to fertilize the spiritual and philosophical life of the West. Modern studies of the rise of colleges and universities in late medieval Europe suggest that in their organization and curricula they were influenced by their Islamic contemporaries. When the famous fifteenth-century Italian humanist Pico della Mirandola reformulated the old Greek maxim about the greatness of man, he expressed it in a characteristic way. 'There is nothing more wonderful on the world's stage than man himself: I have read so in the works of the Arabs.'

In the thirteenth and fourteenth centuries then, in Italy and other parts of Europe, the path was taken which scholars in Baghdad had trodden four hundred years before: the assimilation to a still predominantly religious culture and theocratic rule of classical learning, Hellenism, sceptical and rational science, Neoplatonic philosophy, and even of older magical and gnostic traditions. 'We have heard of late,' wrote Ibn Khaldun in 1377, 'that in Western Europe the philosophical sciences are thriving, their works reviving, their sessions of study increasing, with abundant teachers and students.' The effects of this tremendous psychological shift in Western culture are still with us, dealing a potentially fatal blow to the religious view of the world which had been the controlling ethos in Western society since the Dark Ages, leading ultimately, for good and ill, to the triumph of today's secular civilization. The reason why this did not happen in Islam is one of the most important questions of our time, though outside the scope of a book such as this. It may, though, be relevant to note that the humanistic vision of life and the dictates of the Christian religion, with its determinist view of history, were perhaps at root irreconcilable. But in the contradiction between the two lies the very heart of the West's view of itself, its greatest triumphs and its worst disasters. Through exploring that contradiction it reached sublime heights in art, music and drama which stand comparison with any in the world. And yet perhaps more than any other civilization it fell prey to the deep-rooted contradiction in its character, the perennial Manichaean struggle in its soul which reached its awful climax in Europe in our own time.

A WORLD ELSEWHERE

Until the thirteenth century, the ancient heartland of civilization embraced Islam, India and China. After the devastating Mongol attacks of that time, a series of new Islamic empires arose by the sixteenth century to rule from the gates of Vienna to the mouths of the Ganges: the Turks, the Safavids in Persia, and the Moghuls in India. Limited in land, people and resources, the countries of Western Europe were forced to look the other way, sidestepping the old powers of Asia. Again, we might be tempted to ask whether this was historical accident or destiny, but it was at a most fortuitous point in Asiatic history, at the end of the century which saw the eclipse of the Mongols, that the West 'discovered' the New World. As we understand it now, this was clearly the event on which the whole course of modern Western history rests, an event which opened unimaginable mental horizons and brought undreamed-of wealth flowing back to Europe; indeed perhaps it was, as Adam Smith called it, the greatest event in history. From Mexico to the Andes, the Europeans appropriated the almost limitless resources from the New World, enslaving its peoples and imposing on them its own gods. For the first time in history, one civilization set out deliberately to dismantle and destroy another. Indeed, in Peru and Central America, two of the six original and independent civilizations which had grown up on earth fell victim to the invaders from Europe and their one truth.

With hindsight we can see now that 1492 was a landmark for all the native peoples of the world, for it marked the beginning of a systematic war waged against them by Western arms, religion, and ideology. It marked too, the beginning of their struggle to maintain their traditions, their beliefs and customs, their ways of seeing against the overwhelming impact of Western culture. And five hundred years on the struggle still continues. The conquest was accompanied by an unparalleled loss of life. In the century after Columbus over two-thirds of the native population of the Americas died through disease and violence. Columbus wrote to the Queen of Spain, 'Our European civilization will bring light to the natives in their darkness, but for ourselves we will gain gold and with gold we will be able to do what we want in the world, and bring souls into paradise.'

ENLIGHTENMENT

The discovery of the New World shifted the centre of gravity of the West away from its old heartland in the Mediterranean to the seaboard of north-west Europe, to nations like Holland and England, Protestant and capitalist. The signs had been there, admittedly, long before. The difference between the northern European countries, which were never, or only superficially, Romanized, and the southern Mediterranean lands, is one of the most ancient divides in European history, in language, food, custom, art, religion and much else. With hindsight it was inevitable that the individualistic peoples of north-west Europe would break with the spiritual authority of Rome, and this they did in the Reformation: the Protestants in Britain, Calvinists in Holland, Lutherans in Germany, went their own way, and with that Rome finally lost its cultural leadership of the West, though in the New World and elsewhere in the Age of Exploration it was able to renew and extend its spiritual empire.

At Maldon, a small port on the east coast of England, is a symbol of that Protestant, individualist age, the intact library of a seventeenth-century scholar, Thomas Plume, who endowed the Professorship of Astronomy at Cambridge. And here are more clues to the way the Western view of the world was changing under the influence of individualism and science. Plume's seven thousand books enable us to step back into the intellectual world of the new, secular civilization of the West at the very point of its rise to world dominion. Here are translations of Greek and Arab science. There is Galileo's vision of the cosmos and Descartes, anatomising the marvels of the human body. But the key figure in the new learning was Francis Bacon. For Bacon saw how science and technology would be used in the future to dispossess the other peoples of the planet and to control nature itself. 'Bacon has acted in the field of learning like the political leaders of the greatest Empires,' wrote the Italian philosopher Vico, 'who, when they have attained supreme power in the human sphere, pit their great resources against nature itself.' Bacon now looks like the prophet of our age, stepping out on the road which would eventually lead to world wars, nuclear bombs and environmental crisis.

The fateful implications of this new science were understood by Bacon himself. For if it were true, as he said, that 'henceforth in human affairs what is most useful in practice would also be the most correct in theory,' then truth itself could be defined in terms of utility, not in terms of religion and morals. And so, 'man could become a law unto himself,' as Bacon said, and 'depend no more on God.' It is one of the founding ideas behind our modern, Western, scientific civilization which would go out and exploit and subdue the entire world in the name of that new science.

Now for Westerners life could be seen as a series of phenomena capable of scientific explanation. The earth itself ceased to be sacred. It was subject now to Western definitions of space and time and mapped on a meridian based on Greenwich. When the Chinese were first shown a map of the whole world by the Jesuit Matteo Ricci, they were shaken by the knowledge of these so-called 'barbarians'. 'Up till then,' Ricci said, 'they had printed maps of the world in which China was all,' but when they saw the world so large and China only a corner of it they knew in truth that the world had changed.

AMERICAN INDEPENDENCE

The first political expression of this new knowledge took place not in Europe but in America. Here the huge spaces and the relatively small indigenous population enabled the settler class easily to dispossess the natives and build their new society, their labour needs sustained by slaves from Africa. It is estimated that between the late seventeenth century and early nineteenth, over eleven million black people were shipped from Africa for this purpose, and to further the profits of European manufacturers. It was the greatest forcible movement of population in history. Bacon's utilitarian vision had come about. Not unmindful of the injustice of slavery, Jefferson, Franklin and their fellows nevertheless had Bacon and Hobbes and the stars of the French Enlightenment in their libraries to justify their faith in reason and limited democracy to shape the future, and to bring all, as they hoped, certain inalienable rights to life, liberty and the pursuit of happiness. It was a seductive vision for the poor and downtrodden of Europe. Between the seventeenth and twentieth centuries, millions of Europeans were able to escape the traditional limitations of their own space and freedom, and settle in other people's lands in America and elsewhere in the globe, totally altering the balance of world history, demography and environment.

In America, when Jefferson and the revolutionaries of 1776 devised the great seal for their new Republic, they put on it a motto from the imperial Roman poet Virgil announcing a new order on earth. You can still see it today on every US dollar bill. But the new order was actually based on older ideas. It was based on the possessive individualism which we have traced back to medieval England. It was based too, on the assumed pre-eminence of the white, Christian, Anglo-Saxon races. And those ideas in the hands of limited democracies, run by the property owners and the movers of money, would become the basis of the phenomenal success of the Western powers.

INDUSTRIAL REVOLUTION
AND WORLD COMMERCE

Hitherto most of the great technological advances in history had come from Asia. In the seventeenth century the highest grade steel came from India; so too the best cotton and textile production. China had long been the leader in cast iron technology and many other forms of mass production. But during the eighteenth century the aggressive use of sea power by the maritime countries of north-west Europe enabled them to take over the world's trade, backed up by industrial revolution at home. And a new form of international culture was born in which most of us still live today, manufacturing capitalism: a system sustained by empires and by the exploitation of what has come to be known as the Third World. The industrial city has since spread across the landscape of the world, from the plains of India to the Yellow River in China. The effects on human beings, on the environment and on the biosphere are still being counted. In the nineteenth century, foreign observers were deeply impressed by the heroic materialism of the new Europe. 'This is an extraordinarily talented people,' said a Chinese diplomat of the British. 'How can we continue to call them barbarians, for they have taken on the mantle of civilization?' Some outsiders even argued the spiritual merits of this new form of society. Hu Shih for example defended the materialistic West on the grounds that it was more spiritual than China; for its ideals were 'built on the search for human happiness, and by increasing material well-being, it will also satisfy the spiritual needs of mankind. Through progress in philosophy, religion and ethics, it will overthrow the religions of superstition and bring the greatest happiness to the greater number of people!' Hu Shih wrote in the 1920s, before the Second World War and the violent birth of a new China. But there is no question that his hope is still cherished everywhere in the West, from the corridors of power to the schoolroom. Perhaps he will be proved right.

RECESSIONAL

So now in the early twenty-first century where does Western history stand? Can we really speak of the triumph of Western values across the world, and even if we could, would it be a good thing? Five hundred years on from Columbus, the capital of the West, indeed the capital of the planet, is now in the New World, Washington, DC. The USA is the heir to the Western barbarians of the Dark Ages, sharing their language, culture and religion. The monuments of Washington, Egyptian obelisks, and Greek and Roman temples, proclaim it to be the inheritor of the legacy, not just of Europe but also of the ancient civilizations. Never in history has so much power resided in the hands of one nation. The ideals of this new order are noble ones as Hu Shih recognized. We need only think of the Lincoln memorial, inspired by the Parthenon in Athens, commemorating one who through a brutal civil war held onto the ideals of the European Enlightenment and the French and American revolutions, the belief that all are born equal, with equal rights to freedom and happiness.

But there is another side to the triumph of the West. For the twentieth century saw warfare on an unparalleled scale, fought by Western powers right across the world, directly or by proxy. Most traumatic of all, between 1939 and 1945, in the very heartland of European culture, in the country where Western music and philosophy found its most sublime expression, there was a systematic attempt to exterminate millions of people, based on twisted theories of racial hegemony: an event so horrifying that it beggars belief or description; an event surely inconceivable to the people of the great civilizations of the past. Since then the smaller and poorer nations of the world have found themselves in the middle of the continued rivalry of the great powers; subject first to prolonged and violent assault and plunder, then to an equally prolonged and insistent attempt to sell them Western ideologies and commodities. And from Africa, the heartland of humanity, to Asia and the Americas, all the native cultures of the world have been turned upside down by the impact of the West, for good or ill. In the last forty years, the impact of civilization on the environment has become the greatest issue in history.

If our troubled time has taught us anything, it is not to believe in utopias. But if talk of a 'new order' is to mean anything in this century then perhaps we should look afresh at our history, see it as others see it and question our collective myths and our cherished ideals, perhaps even our notion of freedom itself. Throughout the countries of the rich West there is a growing and profound disquiet: a feeling that the Western way of life itself is no longer supportable, morally or practically, because of pollution, environmental destruction, and the continuing exploitation of the mass of humanity. If that disquiet is justified, which surely it is, then the great question for the next generation is simple. Are the values of the West alone enough to guarantee the continuing health of the planet? Those values as we have seen, are writ large in Western history: individualistic, competitive, acquisitive, always pushing outwards, 'never happy in an empty room,' as Pascal said. And yet it is the bearers of that vision of life, the rulers of the West, who hold in their hands the future of the planet. But perhaps at the very moment of its triumph, the West has reached that point which comes to all civilizations when, to avoid disaster, it must transform itself by learning from others. The crisis of earth and spirit we now face was caused by one form of civilization, that of the West. Perhaps what is needed now is a dialogue with the other peoples and cultures of the world, a dialogue beyond anything seen before. There are signs that this is already happening. And if such a dialogue ever does take place in a real spirit of equality, we can be sure that it will centre on the same fundamental principles which were argued over so long ago in the Axis Age by Confucius, Buddha, and their contemporaries: the conflicting demands of freedom and equality, of the individual and the collective, of the rational and the spiritual.

India, for example, taught long ago that the lust for possession will destroy us, and that life is sacred – all life not just that of humanity. Long ago too the Chinese believed that the basis of life was finding the right harmony between mankind and nature; that we must balance the needs of the individual and of society; that the individual must accept limits on space and desire in a world with finite resources. The civilization of Islam, though the object of much mistrust and little sympathy in the West, also has much to teach the world about the possibility of humanistic values and pluralism and spirituality in a modern society: the value of tradition. These great alternative traditions speak to us now with growing urgency in the aftermath of the destructive twentieth century. And they speak on behalf of the vast majority of the people of the planet; their insights as valuable to life as the rainforests, for these, we might say, are the rainforests of the spirit.

'The goal of civilization,' said the greatest of all historians, the Arab Ibn Khaldun, 'is settled life and the achievement of luxury. But there is a limit which cannot be overstepped. When prosperity and luxury come to a people they are followed by excessive consumption and extravagance.' With that, he says, 'the human soul itself is undermined, both in its worldly well-being and in its spiritual life.'

RETURN TO URUK

There is one last journey in this search for the origins of civilization, a journey back to the starting point, to Southern Iraq, to the Garden of Eden, and to Uruk, the first city on earth. Here the great revolution happened five thousand years ago when people first began to live in cities, in a way of life which now shapes the lives of the mass of the population of the planet. Now Uruk is a lunar wilderness, its once fertile fields ruined by ecological catastrophe. Five thousand years on from the time when civilization first arose here in Iraq, we are still fascinated by the experience of these early people. Not only by their inventiveness, but also, I suspect, by their pessimistic reading of human history; by their struggle to contain war in human life; to find a workable moral law and social order; to preserve the earth.

In our own time we have explored space, and the workings of the mind. But no more than they have we escaped the age-old contract with Mother Earth, which all so-called primitive societies take as granted. Five thousand years ago, with the advent of cities here in Iraq, a fundamental split began in the human psyche; a fundamental realignment of cosmology and technology; a transforming process which resulted in a civilization set apart from nature, run by economic necessities, which superseded older forms of behaviour. In the last hundred years, through the agency of the West, this conception has spread across the planet. Five thousand years on, right across the world, the problems civilization faces are just the same as at its beginning: archaic political institutions through which the few dominate the many; over-population; unequal distribution of the fruits of the earth between rich and poor, and grossly wasteful consumption of those resources by the rich; and the now stark anachronism of the sovereign independent nation state, an idea which seems destined soon to be consigned to the dustbin of history.

The legacy of civilization, a hundred and fifty generations on, is, as the ancient poet of Uruk, the author of the epic of Gilgamesh, dreamed, freeing our imaginations and, potentially, our lives. And yet our material success is now threatening the existence of the species as a whole, and indeed of *all* species, whose own rights now are beginning to assert themselves alongside those much-vaunted rights of man. And there is the conundrum we bequeath our children, and their children, in the twenty-first century.

The ancient Sumerians, the creators of the first civilization, told a wonderful myth about its origins. It was, they said, a devil's bargain. It offered the noblest ideals of humanity but it also brought violence, greed and destruction. All this is civilization, the Sumerian God of Wisdom tells Inanna of Uruk, who will take it back to her city, and thence give it to the world. And if you wish its benefits, he goes on, you must take all its qualities without argument:

... The art of being mighty,
the art of dissimulation,
the art of being straightforward,
the plundering of cities,
the setting up of lamentations,
the rejoicing of the heart.

the craft of the carpenter,
the craft of the copper-worker,
the craft of the scribe,
the craft of the smith,
the craft of the reed-worker.

... the art of being kind,
the kindling of fire ...
the weary arm,
the hungry mouth,
the assembled family,
procreation....

... fear, consternation, dismay,
the kindling of strife,
the soothing of the heart ...

All these things I will give you, holy Inanna, but once you
have taken them, there can be no dispute, and you cannot
give them back.

BIBLIOGRAPHY

This book is adapted from film scripts and writing for pictures is a very different business from writing for the printed page. A book of this nature can best hope to stimulate the reader to look elsewhere; in particular to the scholars on whose work much of this is based – scholars such as Simon Leys, Raymond Dawson and Theodore de Bary on China, Barry Kemp on Egypt, T F Madan on India. Hence this bibliography, which lists the main books I have found useful and interesting.

On Iraq: for obvious reasons there is no good guide book (the old *Guide Bleu* is still the best), but there is an excellent atlas, M Roaf's *A Cultural Atlas of Mesopotamia* (1991). For travellers' tales, try F Stark *Baghdad Sketches* (1937) and *East is West* (1945); E S Stevens *By Tigris and Euphrates* (1922); W Thesiger *The Marsh Arabs* (1964); G Maxwell *A Reed Shaken by the Wind* (1957); G Young *Return to the Marshes* (1977). Among many earlier accounts is W Loftus *Chaldaea and Susiana* (1857). For a basic history: G Roux *Ancient Iraq* (Penguin 1980 ed.). On the romantic story of Iraqi archaeology: Seton Lloyd *Foundations in the Dust* (1980 ed.). For early religion, T Jacobson *The Treasures of Darkness* (1976) is a brilliant synthesis. S N Kramer's *History begins at Sumer* (1981 ed.) and *The Sumerians* (1963) are still classics. References to the site excavations at Uruk, Eridu, Ur, Nippur etc, will be found in these works and in S Lloyd *The Archaeology of Mesopotamia* (1978). On Sumerian literature and poetry: T Jacobson *The Harps that once ...* (1987) and S Dalley *Myths from Mesopotamia* (1989). For general works on the Islamic period: a good introduction is A Hourani *A History of the Arab Peoples* (1989); on medieval Baghdad: G Makdisi *The Rise of Colleges* (1981) and *Religion, Learning and Science – the Abbasid Period* ed. M J L Young and J D Lathan (Cambridge 1990); on the Sufis of Baghdad and Basra good introductions are J Baldick *Mystical Islam* (London 1989) and A Schimmel *Mystical Dimensions of Islam* (1975). M. Momen *Shi'i Islam* (1985) is a good introduction to Shiism, one of many more recent studies, but for accounts of Shia ritual the reader has to turn to older works such as E S Stevens, or D Donaldson *The Shiite*

Religion (1933). On the Mandaeans: E S Drower *The Mandaeans of Iraq and Iran* (1962), K Rudolph *Mandaeism* (1978) and *Gnosis* (1987), which also has a valuable introduction to the Manichaeans. A brilliant guide to the whole period is Peter Brown *The World of Late Antiquity* (1971). J M Wagstaff *The Evolution of Middle Eastern Landscapes* (1985) is a pioneering effort on landscape history from prehistory till the late twentieth century.

On India an excellent paperback collection is *Sources of Indian Tradition* (ed. A T Embree 1988). For a good general introduction see *A History of India* (Penguin 1966) by R Thapar. On prehistory the best guide is B and R Allchin *The Rise of Civilisation in India and Pakistan* (1982); the classic account is *Mohenjo-Daro and the Indus Civilisation* by Sir John Marshall (1931). On Indian art: *In the Image of Man*, Arts Council of Great Britain (1982); *The History of Architecture in India* by C Tadgell (London 1990); *South Indian Bronzes* C Sivaramurti (1981 ed. Delli); S Kramrisch *The Art of India* (Phaidon 1954); P Chandra *The Sculpture of India 3000 BC – 1300 AD* Harvard UP (1985); *Art of the Imperial Cholas* by V Dehejia (1990); *The Raj: India and the British 1600–1947* ed. C Bayley (1990); *Much Maligned Monsters* (1977) by P Mitter is a dazzling look at western reactions to Indian art.

On Hinduism in general there are a number of convenient introductions in paperback, e.g. those by J Brocklebank, R Zaehner, M Biardeau and K Sen; perhaps the best introduction to Hindu polytheism is A Danielou *The Gods of India* (1985 ed.). An excellent guide to wider questions of Indian religion is T F Madan (ed.) *Religion in India* (1991). There are many good accounts of pilgrimage and sacred sites: D Eck *Benares, City of Light* (1983) is outstanding – full of insights; S M Bhardwaj *Hindu Places of Pilgrimage* (1973) is a very useful overview. On language and the Aryan question: J P Mallory *In Search of the Indo-Europeans* (1991): D MacAlpin in *Transactions of the American Philological Society* (Vol 71 pt 3 1981) on Dravidian linguistics. There is a very good introduction to the Sanskrit language *Teach Yourself Sanskrit* by M Coulson (1976). The best guide books to India are the old John Murray series; The *Lonely Planet* guide is useful; *Pakistan Handbook* by Isobel Shaw (1989) is the best for the Indus region.

On China, *Sources of Chinese Tradition* (ed. de Bary 1960) is a brilliant collection; *Imperial China* by Raymond Dawson (1964) a readable and humane introduction; *The Burning Forest* by Simon Leys (1988) an indispensable guide to the modern fate of China's 'great tradition.' *The Legacy of China* (Oxford 1972) ed. R Dawson is a very useful collection of essays on history, art, science and literature which leads the reader on to *Historians of China and Japan* (1961 ed.) W G Beasley and E G Pulleyblank; D Nivison *The Life and Thought of Chang Hsueh Cheng* (1966); M Sullivan *A Short History of Chinese Art* (1967); W Watson *Ancient Chinese Bronzes* (1977 ed.); *Science and Civilisation in China* ed. J Needham (7 vols, 1954). Volume I is an introduction: an abridged edition has also been published. On Chinese prehistory recent indispensable surveys are Li Chi *Anyang* (1977); the *Archaeology of Ancient China* (1986 ed.) and *Shang Civilisation* (1980) both by K C Chang. Paul Unschuld's *Medicine in China* (1985) is a brilliant survey from the Shang to the twentieth century; on food *Food in Chinese Culture* ed K C Chang (1977) is a terrific read; an important aspect of Sung Kaifeng was its restaurant culture: the oldest restaurant in the world is reputed to be Ma Yuxing's Bucket Chicken house in Kaifeng! It is unnecessary to cite individual editions of Confucius and the early philosophers which are all available in paperback; likewise the Tang poets, though a gem is *Late Tang Poets* ed A C Graham (Penguin 1965). Most of the great Sung writers are poorly represented in English, though the *Literary works of Ou-Yang Hsiuh (1007–72)* by R Egan (1984), helps to fill a major gap. On European relations with China are Nigel Cameron *Barbarians and Mandarins* (1989 ed.) and Jerome Chen *China and the West* (1979). A readable survey of later Chinese history is J Spence *The Search for Modern China* (1990). On the origin of cities in China, but relevant to all the chapters in this book, is *The Pivot of the Four Quarters* by Paul Wheatley (1971). Atlases: *A Cultural Atlas of China* ed. C Blunden and M Elvin, and *The Contemporary Atlas of China* ed N Sivin, F Wood, P Brooke and C Ronan (1988) are excellent. Lastly, for an exciting overview of the Chinese great tradition, see *East Asian Civilisations* by T de Bary (1988) whose brilliant final chapter shaped my ideas, for example, on Zheng He's voyages (see page 105). See now too the *Blue Guide to China* by F Wood.

On Egypt there are many good general introductions, such as T G H James *Ancient Egypt* (1988) and J Baines and J Malek *The Atlas of Ancient Egypt*. This bibliography concentrates on the early and late periods: M Hoffman *Egypt before the Pharaohs* (1980) and Walter Emery *Archaic Egypt* (1961) are indispensable, along with a fine overview by Barry Kemp *Ancient Egypt: Anatomy of a Civilisation* (1989). For the Hellenistic age: *Egypt after the Pharaohs* by Alan Bowman (1986) and *Hellenism in Late Antiquity* by G Bowerstock (1990). *The Egyptian Hermes* by Garth Fowden (1986) is a fascinating study of late Egyptian paganism: the continuity of such ideas into the early Islamic period is not a part of Fowden's book, but it is fascinating that the early Sufi alchemist and mystic, Dhu'n-Nun (d. 859) for example also came from Akhmim: see Schimmel *Mystic Dimensions of Islam*. There are two delightful studies by N Lewis: *Greeks in Ptolemaic Egypt* (1986) and *Life in Egypt under Roman Rule* (1983). On the art of the late period there is a fine exhibition catalogue: *Cleopatra's Egypt* Brooklyn Museum 1988. On the survival of ancient customs: E W Lane *The Modern Egyptians* (1836) and *The Ancient Egyptians* by R David (1982). The best guide books to Egypt are still old Baedekers.

Central America: there are many popular works available. N Hammond *Ancient Maya Civilisation* (1982) and *Religion and Empire* by G W Conrad and A A Demarest (1984) are both very good, so too is the *Atlas of Ancient America* by M Coe, D Snow and E Benson. There are a number of recent works linking past and present here: *The View from the Top of the Temple* by K Pearce (1984), *Time and the Highland Maya* by Barbara Tedlock (1982) and *The Daykeeper* by B N and L M Colby (1981). On the Spanish impact: *Ambivalent Conquests* by I Clendinnen (1987) and *Maya Society Under Colonial Rule* by N M Farriss (1984). On the recent situation, *Garrison Guatemala* by G Black (1984) is one of many. More recently Ronald Wright has written *Time Among the Maya* (1989), a marvellous book of travels in Belize, Guatemala and Mexico, recommended to all who would journey in search of the Maya universe: on no account to be missed! Lastly Dennis Tedlock with the help of Andres Xiloj has translated the Mayan genesis: *Popol Vuh* (1985), a must!

Since the first edition of this book was published, I have written one or two studies of particular aspects treated in this book, which the reader may find helpful. On the Greek adventure in Asia, *In the Footsteps of Alexander the Great* (2004 ed.); on the civilizations of Mexico and Peru, and the European impact, *Conquistadors* (2000), which has an extensive bibliography of source material on the events of the sixteenth century and their continuing legacy. For a present-day snapshopt of the Tamil civilization in Chapter 2, see my *Smile of Murugan: A South Indian Journey* (2001 ed.).

I have not thought it necessary to add a western bibliography, but *The Times Atlas of World History* and *Past Worlds: The Times Atlas of Archaeology* (1995) are a constant source of ideas. I leave the last word to Chang Hsueh Cheng, who in 1797 wrote 'A century hence, we too will be men of old. Let us therefore put ourselves in their place. How then will it fare with us?'

PICTURE CREDITS

All photographs by Michael Wood except:

Picture section 1
Page 1 (above) Georg Gerster/Network Photographers
Page 2 (above) akg-images/Erich Lessing
Page 3 Robert Harding Picture Library
Page 5 (below) The Trustees of the Chester Beatty Library, Dublin
Page 8 (below) Mary Evans Picture Library

Picture section 2
Page 1 (above) akg-images/François Guenet
Page 1 (below) akg-images/François Guenet
Page 2 (below) British Museum
Page 3 (below):akg-images/Erich Lessing
Page 4 (above) Royal Geographical Society, London
Page 8 akg-images

ACKNOWLEDGEMENTS

This book is the product of journeys going back over several years, and it is a happy task to thank some of the people who made it possible. Starting in Iraq: Kamil Alwan Shihab for sharing his knowledge (and good humour) over our weeks together; Muklus, Mersin and Falah our drivers for their constant care and friendship; Muhar Abu Gumar for our many memorable days at Warka; Dr Joseph Habbi in Mosul, and the al-Mulla family in Irbil. Thanks too go to the religious authorities at Kerbala, and especially to the Gailani family in Baghdad for generously allowing free access to their great shrine and its library. The Mandaean community in Baghdad were unfailingly hospitable, as were the Yezidis at Sheikh Adi, where I will never forget a magnificent meal in the open air in that once idyllic spot. I am grateful to the American and British schools in Baghdad for their help: in particular to Tony Wilkinson, Erica Hunter, Jeremy Black and Georgina Hermann; also to Prof. R Boehmer at Warka. Many Iraqi friends abroad were unstinting in their help – especially Dr Lamia al-Gailani.

In India, first in Tamil Nadu: I am grateful to the directors of the museums in Madras and Tanjore; to M. Nagaratinam and her family for their continuing friendship and hospitality and also for our many journeys to Tamil holy sites; to R.N. Dikshithar and all the priests of the Nataraja temple at Chidambaram; to the temple authorities of the Minakshi temple in Madurai for their special kindness; also the committees at the Jambukesvara and Ramanathasvami temples for allowing a non-Hindu access to their shrines; S Natarajan, 'parish priest' at Konerirajapuram; the priests at the Thyagaraja temple in Tiruvarur; in Madras thanks as always to S. Kannan and to Sushila Ravindranath. In Calcutta the staff of the Asiatic Society spared no pains on our behalf. A belated thanks too to Jyoti Maya Datta and family. In Benares my special thanks go to Col. V.P. Singh (Retd) for being an exemplary guide to his city and for sharing his reminiscences of his own family traditions; also to Ganesh Pandy and his family who have been mahants there for at least four centuries. In Allahabad I would like to thank Rustom and Shernaz Gandhi and their staff, for their help and kindness over several visits to the Hotel Finaro – surely the nicest hotel in India! In Pakistan, I am most grateful to the Archaeological Service and the Ministry of Tourism for their solicitude during my visit to Mohenjo-Daro.

In China: in Qufu Mr Guo shared his deep knowledge of Confucius' home town and its history, ancient and modern. In Xian thanks to Lao Kung and also to Ms Suen; our driver Mr Yu was an unfailing source of strength and fun one hot June when Lao Kung took us down the Yellow River; to the Imam of the Grand Mosque in Xian for his hospitality and wisdom; to the abbot of Xingjiose monastery; to Sam Lieu and Peter Bryder, who sent me to the Cao'an temple near Quenzhou, the last Manichaean temple in the world; Yang Hsi-chang at Anyang; the manager and staff of the Taishan Hotel, Tai'an; but most of all thanks to He Yuxie for making my visits to China in 1990 so memorable.

In Egypt my special thanks to Hamdi Mohammed Mosa and his family in Luxor, to Haggag el Sanousy, and Mohammed Khalid abu Zed and their families for their matchless hospitality. Thanks also to the staff of the Pharaohs Hotel in Luxor for taking such good care of us on a long stay; to the custodians of Abu'l Haggag's mosque in Luxor, to the abbot and monks of St Paul's monastery, and to the religious authorities at the Al Ahzar mosque in Cairo.

In Central America Jim Conroy taught me more than he could ever realize as he shared his experiences there during our journeys through Guatemala; Andres Xiloj at Barrio St Isabel, Momostenango, showed this gringo some of the ancient rituals and traditions of the Highland Maya in a most generous and open-hearted way, for which I will remain ever grateful to him. Professor Dennis Tedlock made our meeting possible. The archaeological services in Guatemala and Honduras were particularly helpful and courteous. On the road in Guatemala, thanks to Vinny, a tower of strength. In Mexico I would like to thank Professor Roberto Galliegos for giving of his time and knowledge in Teotihuacan and allowing access to the sacred cave. In Europe, Dr Gianni Ponti in

Rome, and Hara Palamidi and Myron Papadakis in Athens were both friends and guides for which much thanks.

At Central TV, Richard Creasey was the 'onlie begetter' of the project and Roger James saw it through with a patience and kindness rare in today's world; to both my thanks. On the other side of the Atlantic, Leo Eaton at Maryland Public TV was a stalwart supporter who kept asking the questions which needed to be asked and gave unstintingly all through the long period of editing when his heart must often have been elsewhere: to Leo (and Gerry), again, thank you. I am grateful also too Jennifer Lawson at Public TV in Washington for her faith in the project. The main film crew which shot *Legacy* was three people: Peter Harvey, Lynette Frewin and Mike Claydon. We trekked together from Jarrow to Baghdad and on to South China and I cannot sufficiently express my debt to them for their skill, stamina and good humour. Sanjiv Talreja and Fredy George shot the episode in India and did a wonderful job; so too did Ray Kawata, Bill Bealmear and Carole Everson from MPT who shot the Central American film. Thanks to Hal Lindes and Ed Wynne, who composed the music. The films were edited by Mark and Paul Brown and by Stephen Griffiths and Annie Moore: their commitment and skill were second to none; their patience and freshness over such a long edit nothing short of miraculous! I should also like to thank this book's editor, Julia Wigg, for her invaluable help with the manuscript. Last of all I want to thank the two people with whom I spent much of the last four years preparing, filming and editing the *Legacy* series. Peter Spry-Leverton produced and directed the films with great expertise, but also with enviable calmness – even when threatened with the destruction of his film by one security apparatchik! Without him *Legacy* would not have made it to the screen. Chris Ledger, the associate producer and researcher, was a never-failing source of support, enthusiasm and good cheer, in addition to his own special skills. To both my heartfelt thanks!

INDEX